Turning Talents into Strengths

Stories of Coaching Transformation

Rhonda Knight Boyle, LLC
PO Box 893159
Oklahoma City, Oklahoma 73159
www.RhondaBoyle.com

Turning Talents into Strengths / Rhonda Knight Boyle

ISBN 978-1-948752-00-8

Turning Talents into Strengths Chapter Four/ Finding Forward

ISBN: 978-1-948752-04-6 / Alicia Santamaria

Turning Talents into Strengths

Stories of Coaching Transformation

Compiled and Edited By

Rhonda Knight Boyle

Rhonda Knight Boyle, LLC
OKLAHOMA CITY, OKLAHOMA

This Book is Dedicated to Coaches Everywhere
Who Maximize Human Potential

*If human beings are perceived as potentials rather
than problems, as possessing strengths instead of
weaknesses, as unlimited rather than dull and
unresponsive, then they thrive and grow
to their capabilities.*

— Barbara Bush

TABLE OF CONTENTS

Turning Talents into Strengths

About the Compiler & Editor - Rhonda Knight Boyle. 13

Introduction - Rhonda Knight Boyle. 15

Chapter One - Joanna Wiesinger, Ph.D. - *Thrive with Strengths* 19

Chapter Two - Marcia Buzzella - *Strengths Empowerment*. 31

Chapter Three - Heidi Convery - *Flourish Through Strengths*. 45

Chapter Four - Alicia Santamaria - *Finding Forward*. 59

Chapter Five - David G. Boop, Ed.D. 75

Career Coaching in the Twenty-First Century

Chapter Six - Kathie Gautille - *Passion and Purpose Bring Life* 87

Chapter Seven - Beverly Griffeth-Bryant - *Drive to Design and Engage*. . .99

Chapter Eight - Murray Guest - *Be Inspired Through Strengths* 111

Chapter Nine - Donna Marie Gardner, M.A. - *Leap of Faith* 125

Chapter Ten - Pia Jansson - *Connecting to Possibilities*. 137

Chapter Eleven - Ken Barr Jr. - *Exceptional Talents*. 149

Chapter Twelve - Debby Rauch Lissaur, CPCC .161

Understanding Colleagues & Accelerating Performance

References 175

Appendix 177

TURNING TALENTS INTO STRENGTHS

About the Compiler & Editor

Rhonda Knight Boyle

Ideation®, Woo®, Maximizer®, Communication®, Activator®

Rhonda Knight Boyle is a transformational leader and her coaching and consulting company utilizes CliftonStrengths® strategies to achieve breakthrough transformation and maximize productivity in individuals, teams and organizations. Rhonda teaches her strengths-based processes through workshops, corporate education, and group coaching.

Rhonda is a strengths evangelist. She writes and speaks prolifically about living a life of contribution using your innate, natural talents. She is the co-host of the Strengths Activation Show that broadcasts weekly on Facebook LIVE, interviewing everyday people and coaches on their talent development. She is an enthusiastic advocate of positive, strengths-based psychology and has been part of the strengths movement since 2008.

You can reach Rhonda at:

Website: www.RhondaBoyle.com
Email: Rhonda@RhondaBoyle.com

Rhonda Knight Boyle

INTRODUCTION

My father passed away in 2005. After the funeral, friends and family went home and my siblings and I went through a box of memorabilia. It had papers, documents, and old photos inside and I found my 2nd grade report card.

I discovered I had UNSATISFACTORY marks for behavior!

"She can't sit still," said one notation. "And she won't stop talking," said another. At the bottom of the report card the teacher had penned, "Rhonda is not living up to her full potential!"

Now, I'm sure I didn't know what potential was, nor could I have spelled it. But already - at seven years old - I was being labeled and put into a box.

How many of you grew up feeling the same? How many of you had bad reports in your parent/teacher conferences? How many of you were judged throughout your childhood because you couldn't sit still, or you wiggled too much? Or maybe you were too quiet and shy? Or maybe you were too smart and nerdy?

And even if you were one of the smart kids who studied hard and graduated with honors, didn't you feel odd, too?

I'm pretty sure that every one of us has grown up believing that we were deficient in one way or another. Through our cultural conditioning, we've tried endlessly to "fix" ourselves. After all, we've been told throughout our childhood and into our adult life that we were not good enough. Most of us have lived a life of comparison, constantly focused on what everyone else is doing and trying to measure up. This is our common experience, growing up in a culture that is satisfied with nothing less than perfection.

A few years after I discovered that report card, I was invited to take the CliftonStrengths® assessment and it literally changed the way I look at myself. I now recognize that as a young student, even as my teachers were trying to form me into their own vision of a model student, the seeds of strength had already been planted. These were natural talents that I was born with and that I developed over time into strengths through natural development.

Instead of talking too much, I learned I am a gifted speaker and writer with the CliftonStrengths® talent of Communication®. Instead of not being able to sit still, I am a catalyst for change who seizes opportunities with my talent theme of Activator®.

I have more talents in my CliftonStrengths® profile, of course. And when I use them in strength, they bring me energy, improve my well-being, and increase my productivity. I contribute to my team, to my work, and to my family in ways that no one on earth can do!

What a shame that I didn't recognize my own talents, my own strength and power, until I was 50-something! How much more could I have contributed to the world had I known this at seven or seventeen? How much more could I have given had my parents and teachers understood how I was uniquely gifted, and guided me in the development of those gifts?

This is why I believe this little test, the CliftonStrengths® assessment, is the most powerful personal and professional development tool on the market today. In my experience, it brings hope. It brings ease. It restores the natural order to your world and mine by allowing people to live, grow, thrive and excel through their own natural gifts and talents.

I am delighted to introduce you a dozen powerful, passionate strengths coaches who have their own stories of discovery, understanding and growth. Not only have they experienced transformation their own lives as a result of the strengths movement, they have touched thousands of others, collectively.

They've helped their clients, students, and employees discover their natural talents and shifted the way they look at themselves. They've focused on what's RIGHT with people, instead of becoming fixated on what's wrong with them.

And isn't this as it should be?

At the heart of this book is the belief that each person is unique and has something to give to the world around us. And while they each work in different areas of business and community, each of these strengths coaches brings the fullness of who they are to the people they serve.

In their own words, let's listen as these amazing coaches tell their stories.

Chapter One - Joanna Wiesinger, Ph.D.

....

THRIVE WITH STRENGTHS

Before I started the CliftonStrengths® journey, my mind and time were focused on two things, my career as a scientist and my family. I was committed to both with passion and excellence. What I didn't know then was that starting the CliftonStrengths® journey would add texture, depth, and more fun to my life!

I am a Ph.D. inorganic chemist by training. I spent many years investing in the scientist-in-me by going through a rigorous graduate program, then working for a chemical company, and surrounding myself with bright scientific minds. Recently, my kids asked me to show them my Ph.D. thesis. As I dusted it off and read its intimidatingly long title about the synthesis of metal complexes containing an annulene ligand, my heart skipped a beat. I remembered how much I loved my time in the lab doing research - by myself, away from people, just "my" chemicals and me.

However, much to my surprise, that all changed seemingly overnight a few years into my career. My desire to become a mom became stronger than my drive to be the next Madame Curie, so I chose to take an early retirement from my company. I decided to stay at home with my kids for what turned out to be over ten years.

Leaning into Discontent

In the first six months post-retirement, I felt very torn between missing my work and colleagues and enjoying my kids and the peaceful home I was creating with my husband. That tug of war became a "whisper of discontent" that was very unsettling. It continues to be a part of my daily life, except now I lean into it because I know why it's there in the first place.

It turns out that I've been hard-wired to achieve, work hard, and push myself to be the very best every single day. I've known that intuitively all my life. It wasn't until I read my CliftonStrengths® results that I had words to express why I was satisfied only when I was "number one." Apparently, my Achiever® and Activator® talent themes are responsible for that!

That "aha" moment happened to me nearly 12 years ago. A friend of mine, now a Gallup-Certified Strengths coach himself and a published author of Strengths Based Marriage (Evans & Kelsey, 2016), introduced my husband and me to the CliftonStrengths® assessment. I loved it right away. It put into words what I already sensed: I was strong! I was unique! I was needed!

The big idea behind the strengths movement resonated with me. Yes, to focusing on what's strong with us! No, to fixating on what's wrong with us! Understanding how I was wired was permitting me to do what I longed to do all along, focus on my personal strengths and others', tapping into the magic that's in all of us, our own "superpowers."

Therefore, I began my self-discovery journey at the ripe age of 40 something. Right away, I realized that when one is wired like me, wired to act first, think second, it feels like hard work to slow down, push the proverbial pause button, and reflect. However, I was undeterred by hard work, and today I am glad that I invested some reflection time early on. It formed the needed foundation for my journey of thriving daily with my strengths.

The first thing that jumped out at me as I analyzed my talents was that I am an influencer or simply put, a "sneezer." What I mean by that is that whatever is on my radar, I want others infected with it. I "sneeze" my excitement all around me, with a full expectation that others will "catch" what I have!

Investing in Talents

The reason why I get energized by inspiring others into action is that most of my dominant talents fall in the Influencing Domain (Rath & Conchie, Strengths Based Leadership: Great Leaders, Teams, and Why People Follow, 2008). I get excited about infusing others with the confidence I have in them to tackle assignments, spearhead projects, or play critical positions on a team. I naturally see strengths in others and enjoy using my strengths to fill gaps in theirs. No wonder that I've felt all along that what I do best is develop leaders. Pouring into leaders who have a full sphere of influence always seemed like my best contribution to others.

I remember exhaling the breath that I apparently held all my life when I read in my results about the Maximizer® talent, "Study success...focus on strengths...seek roles in which you are helping people succeed." That I could do!

With the passion and resolve that have always been my hallmark, I made an intentional decision to get better at developing leaders. The profound words that, "leading others isn't just a way of thinking or acting, it's a way of communicating" guided my next steps (Sinek, 2014).

I needed to refine my natural command of the spoken word. I chose to do that by joining a local Toastmasters® club. Every week, I was prodded out of my comfort zone to give a talk and then listen to constructive feedback. That one hour a week was simultaneously the best and the worst hour of my week. Speaking in front of others is no joke! I saw results; I was getting better at landing my ideas on others.

Another natural talent of mine is collecting ideas and books. Since I wanted to acquire new knowledge in how to lead others better, I needed to get some fresh insights.

I asked my husband, a seasoned businessman, to give me his best business "picks" on this topic. I read the books, and then he and I discussed them, refining our ideas in the process.

Next, I practiced being a developer of leaders both frequently and intentionally. I sought out new leadership roles in my community, my school district, and my church. As I grew my talents into strengths and then connected these strengths to the things that were impacting the lives of others, I felt more satisfied than ever before. I felt alive!

Becoming the Coach

Looking back, I can see that the timing of my intentional investment in strengths was divinely appointed. You see, I was about to face a new season in my personal life. My three kids were happily pursuing their big dreams, and my husband and I were becoming empty nesters.

I remember feeling a bit disoriented as I acknowledged a pang of urgency to find a new outlet for my interests and freshly discovered strengths. Chemistry no longer had my heart. I was looking for something new.

One day, I found an email in my inbox from my husband who was away on a business trip. It simply read, "This might interest you, love!" The email was an invitation from Gallup® to "become an elite strengths coach with Gallup® certification."

It was the second time in my life that I exhaled a breath that I had held for a very long time. Yes! I knew right away that becoming a strengths coach was for me. It would marry my passion for inspiring others and pointing them to what they do best! It would give me a new tool for developing leaders and their teams.

I took a day to learn more about the course and discuss it with my husband. We saw no red flags. I signed up for the class within a week, and a month later I opened my coaching firm, Thrive with Strengths.

The name of my company reflects the vision I have as a coach. I want to help others thrive with their strengths daily. It is that simple. Specifically, I want to help leaders and their teams to identify, maximize, and leverage what they naturally do better than anyone else, so they can have more significant impact on others.

Recognizing the Talents

Doing that as a strengths coach has been a lot of fun. I get a front row seat to countless "aha" moments from the leaders in my life. One of them came from a passionate and savvy business owner, a busy mother of four.

Our session started on an upbeat note as we looked carefully at her results. However, something shifted when we came to her Activator® talent theme. She felt this was the very talent that stood in her way of being more productive in life.

My client confessed how she often started projects but didn't finish them, how she impatiently got new things off the ground but hardly ever brought them to landing, and how she took ideas and put them into action but had no desire to see them come to fruition. I could tell that this strong leader was feeling inadequate in her role as a team manager.

I asked her if it was essential to her job that she is the one finishing, landing, and closing the projects. She paused to ponder my question. Then she looked up with a glint in her eyes. She could think of at least one colleague on her team who was the "finisher." Maybe he could complete the projects she gets off the ground.

Within the span of our session, my client went from thinking that there was something wrong with her to seeing that there was something powerful about the talent she was bringing to her team. Her lane was to launch projects by bringing everyone else to the "START."

I checked on this amazing leader a month later. She was in the process of handing over a critical project to her colleague. Her voice was upbeat. She felt energized by collaborating with others and letting them flex their strengths muscles, while she was staying true to herself.

Melting the Tension

Just a few months later, on a sunny afternoon, I met with two young leaders for a very different coaching session.

This married couple was in a busy season with four small children and a successful home-based business. When I asked them what they wanted to get out of our "strengths in marriage" session, their answer was quick and concise. Their goal was to understand how they could support each other better. They felt that their strengths were the source of tension between them.

I chose to focus on two things during our time together. We zeroed in on what their respective strengths brought to their marriage as well as what they needed from each other. As I asked questions and the couple talked, I could tell the relationship-building husband was starting to lean in a little closer to his strategically thinking wife. There was some definite melting of the hearts taking place.

Not even 24 hours later, I received an update from the couple. They already debriefed what they had learned about each other the day before. They did that by posing a compelling question to themselves, "Since we know our needs, what must we do to cultivate a marriage in which those needs are met, and our strengths reach the levels we desire?" They even wrote up a list of action items for each of their respective strengths. They committed to carrying them out for a month before regrouping again. Wow, I was impressed with my leaders' focus and intentionality!

As they thanked me for my encouragement and insight, I was electrified by the visible shift in their perspective. The initial question of "what's wrong with us?" was now rephrased into "how do we reach for what's strong with us?"

Embracing the Differences

When my son was 15-years-old, I asked him to take the CliftonStrengths® assessment. I needed more insight into my young man's mind. I was concerned with his propensity to be stuck in the mire of indecision. Daily, I seemed to tell him, "Just make up your mind, please. You have all the data!" Spoken like a true scientist with a bias towards action and swift decision-making, right?

The moment I read my son's results, it felt as if the scales fell from my eyes. There was nothing wrong with my son! The very things that drove me crazy were not my son's weaknesses, but his strengths. They were different from mine, all in the Strategic Thinking Domain (Rath & Conchie, Strengths Based Leadership: Great Leaders, Teams, and Why People Follow, 2008), so I mistook them for weaknesses.

I promptly apologized to my deep thinker, "Will you please forgive me? I completely misunderstood you." My son looked at me thoughtfully and answered simply, "That's okay, Mom. I know who I am."

That moment changed me forever. These days, I give my son ample time to think so that I honor his need to deliberate and examine situations from every angle. He rewards me with an occasional grunt and a smile.

Dialing the Strengths

That moment also impacted me as a coach. It reminded me to approach every new client with a curious and open-mindset, free of any preconceived notions. This reminder was especially helpful when I led a workshop for some 60 educators earlier this year.

Early on in the workshop, a fantastic teacher and a team lead was describing how much she loved her talent themes of Discipline®, Consistency®, and Achiever®. She felt they made her inherently intense and very productive. Daily she would plan her work carefully and then work her plan meticulously. She wrote the hashtags #cant-stop #wontstop on her paper and proudly looked at her teammates.

This brand new team was facing a challenge. How could they move forward, honoring each other's different talents and still be highly productive? I heard concern, and I even saw some tears. I knew it was my time to step in. I drew a simple picture of an old-fashioned radio with five dials, each dial representing a top talent. I explained how when we understand our strengths, we are in control of them, dialing them up or down depending on the situation. I asked each member of the team to study their respective talents and then start making necessary and intentional dial adjustments. I assured them that the process would work, though it might feel awkward at first, a weak muscle being stretched and pulled to grow stronger.

It will be a few months before I work with these leaders again; I don't know the end of this story. However, I could sense a resolve in the team to keep learning about each other's filters. I felt that was a great start to their strengths journey.

Healing through Coaching

In my experience, there are many reasons why a person starts on the path of learning about their strengths. Sometimes they feel like it's their last resort, having tried many other tools. That's what happened to my friend. And it all started with her unexpected text.

She sounded desperate. She was disoriented by years of striving and failing to juggle what she wanted out of life. She desired a thriving career, an intimate marriage, and happy kids. She felt tired, discouraged, and defeated.

When we met for the first time, I promised to come alongside her as a friend and a strengths coach. I asked her to take the CliftonStrengths® assessment, of course. I knew that focusing on her inherent strengths would be a significant first step towards healing.

I can still remember the day we met to go over my friend's assessment results. She came prepared, having highlighted words and phrases that resonated with her. She was alert and full of insightful questions. It felt to me like she was reviving parts of her that became stale or maybe hidden and forgotten.

We met for coaching sessions every month for exactly a year. My friend was a quick study. She grasped the power of aiming her natural talents at the many challenges in her life. She courageously brought what was strong about her to her marriage, her kids, and her job. She worked hard to silence the "old tape" of "What's wrong with me?" and "Why can't I get this right?" I watched her become a vibrant wife, mom, and an engaged leader.

This leader's fantastic journey to feeling herself again started with a brave first step to being vulnerable and open to coaching. She understood that she needed something like the CliftonStrengths® assessment. And she needed someone like me, a coach, to hold up a mirror and say, "This is who you are! Strong! Unique! Capable!"

Thriving with Strengths Daily

I am convinced that is the reason why millions of people have taken the CliftonStrengths® assessment to date. We resonate with the idea that "speaking" a common language of strengths is healing.

The reality is that our differences in gender, skin color, culture, or education introduce us to each other before we even have a chance to say a word. Our strengths step in to build a bridge between us, making our differences much less important.

In the last 12 years of my own strengths journey, I have seen the power of investing skills, knowledge, and practice into developing our inherent talents. The more we grow our talents into strengths, the more impact we have on others. It's that simple and it's that powerful!

No wonder that Tom Rath, author of StrengthsFinder 2.0, recently said to a room full of coaches, *"Life is about connecting strengths to the things that will change the lives of others."* Absolutely!

The more each of us thrives with our strengths, the more we increase our contribution to others making a difference in their lives. What do you want to contribute to others using your talents?

I have a desire to see a strengths-based world one day. A strengths-based world that's resolute in rephrasing the ineffective question of "What's wrong with us?" to the empowering and healing question of "What's strong with us?"

A strengths-based world that believes our greatest contribution will always come from our strengths, not our weaknesses. A strengths-based world that freely offers its strengths to others and in return sees increased engagement, accountability, and performance.

I have a desire to see the world THRIVE WITH STRENGTHS daily and have more fun in the process!

ABOUT THE AUTHOR

Joanna Wiesinger, Ph.D.

Maximizer®, Achiever®, Input®, Communication®, Activator®

Joanna Wiesinger is a contribution coach who helps leaders and their teams leverage what they naturally do best for greater impact. Joanna is a Gallup-Certified Strengths Coach, Ph.D. chemist, frequent speaker, published author, and leadership catalyst.

She offers one-on-one coaching, team workshops, and corporate training using the CliftonStrengths® based approach. Joanna helps her clients find the right conditions to Thrive with Strengths daily.

You can reach Joanna at:

Website: www.thrivewithstrengths.com
Email: joanna@thrivewithstrengths.com
LinkedIn: www.linkedin.com/in/joannawiesinger

TURNING TALENTS INTO STRENGTHS

Chapter Two - Marcia Buzzella

···

STRENGTHS EMPOWERMENT

In addition to serving as a coach and mentor, I am a software quality assurance professional and information technology manager. With an undergraduate degree in accounting, I thought my career path involved becoming a Certified Public Accountant. Instead, I stumbled upon the software testing industry, and I decided to pursue auditing insurance and finance software rather than accounts. I recently left an outstanding company, where I led the software testing practice, to move across the country in support of my husband's career. Together we are writing the next chapter of our respective careers.

While on the phone with a coach helping him update his resume, my husband called me into the room to ask if I'd ever heard of the CliftonStrengths® assessment. I had not, so we put the coach on speakerphone to find out more. In the hours and months that followed, we learned about our talents gaining a better understanding how to support one another. Our top talents, which center around thinking and achieving, came as no surprise. Family and friends know us as the couple that gets things done and makes things happen. The most significant revelation for us uncovered Significance® in my most dominant talents. As we delved into the nuances of the theme, I found myself nodding in agreement with every statement that I read.

Motivated by the perceptions of others … yes! A constant yearning to be and do more. Absolutely! Learning the characteristics of this strength helped my husband understand what he perceived as odd quirks in my behavior.

Clarity also emerged by comparing our dominant influencing talents. The drive fostered by his Competition® talent is mostly internal and prompted by comparison. The motivation cultivated by my Significance® talent is sparked via external perceptions. Once we discovered the internal and external factors of these talents, we could easily see why what worked for him did not work for me and vice versa.

Discovering my dominant talents reinforced what I already knew about myself. I take my responsibilities seriously, thrive on achieving goals (large or small), and love learning as much as I can along the way. When I identified the talent of Relator® as one of my strongest themes, the universe started to make more sense. Meeting new people and making new friends is not an effortless process for me. Shy and reserved, I tend to watch and listen before acting. Occasionally, opportunities would pass before I mustered the energy to move. In my mind, I rationalized my behavior as the cost of being introverted and accepted it as a personality flaw. What a relief to learn that it was actually a potential gift!

As I continued to dig more, I learned that my actions were grounded in risk minimization rather than shyness. I value all my relationships and take full responsibility for being a good spouse, daughter, friend, mentor, and co-worker. Investing in a relationship comes with personal costs and risks. When I commit, I commit fully. I now under-stand that when I failed to speak up, I was not gathering my courage but assessing whether I could bring my authentic self to the table. Once I understood this distinction, I could prepare more effectively for diverse types of interactions.

Knowledge is power. Now that I am aware of my natural talents, I can assess circumstances through a more compelling, personalized lens.

For example, I love to gather new information and believe it is my responsibility to share this knowledge with others, as appropriate. Sharing experience requires me to set aside my introverted tendencies in favor of actively seeking opportunities to engage with individuals and teams. Accomplishing these tasks, by expanding my comfort zone, is incredibly satisfying and knowing that the achievements occur because of my unique strengths is wonderfully empowering.

The Call to Coach

The call to formal coaching snuck up on me while I indulged my life-long learner cravings by earning a doctoral degree. Helping others grow personally and professionally will always be my favorite part of leadership, but I had not considered becoming a coach. The desire to coach emerged from the synergies between my dissertation research and my eagerness to help individuals and teams successfully complete software development projects.

After earning some bumps and bruises in the software quality assurance world, I realized that history repeats itself all too often in this industry. Scrapped projects. Delayed deployments. Test documents sent to live customers. Shortened timelines. Critical defects introduced to production. As a leader, I watched as individuals encountered the same challenges I lived through repeatedly. Why were the problems of the past still plaguing today's teams?

Determined to answer this question, and to help software test professionals move beyond these obstacles, I went back to school to earn a Doctor of Business Administration degree, with a specialization in Leadership. For my dissertation, I elected to dig into the human factors associated with opportunities and challenges in the software testing industry.

I spent the next three years wading through books and articles, interviewing software test professionals, and analyzing the data gathered. The core takeaway from this endeavor was the premise that successful IT projects occur when teams possess a balance of social and technical skills. I also discovered that the soft skills of communication, problem solving, and adaptability allow software test professionals to influence the success of IT projects.

Eager to share my findings, I presented the information to small groups of IT project stakeholders. At the end of the first session, a Quality Assurance manager posed a question that crashed my thought processes completely. He asked, "How do you evaluate your soft skills so that you know where to start?" Upon reflection, I realized that I described a perfect destination but offered no means to arrive at paradise.

Around that same time, I engaged a strengths coach for personal development. I had already been using the perspective gained from reflecting on my talents to review my performance and identify growth opportunities. However, this time I needed outside help. Completing my degree left me feeling adrift, and I needed perspective. Little did I know the two paths would quickly converge.

Soft skills are inherently personal. The social capabilities that make one person successful may not apply to another individual. Similarly, an individual's talent themes are unique. The odds of another person having the same top five talents (in the same order) is 1 in 34,000,000. Enter the strengths-based coaching perspective for personal development and soft skill improvement. Within just a few months, I became a Gallup-Certified Strengths Coach and began helping individuals and teams identify, appreciate, and focus their talents while enhancing their social capabilities.

The Next Level

One of my most rewarding coaching experiences was with an IT professional with 15 years' experience. She approached me to help her "make a radical move" that would "elevate" her to the next level. Her plate overflowed with opportunity, and she was attempting to juggle it all. She was expending a lot of effort without realizing tangible progress. Lack of advancement, in addition to frustrations stemming from organizational politics, caused depression and apathy to form. She knew something had to change and that she needed help fast.

The results of her CliftonStrengths® assessment gave us a great deal of perspective. Exploring each of her dominant talents provided key revelations and enabled us to view her situation differently. Her talent theme of Connectedness® caused her to associate the plethora of tasks overflowing her list of responsibilities with one another. As a result, her Futuristic® talent and her vision of success required completing all the activities currently in flight. What an impossible and thankless task!

I invited her to create a list of her personal and professional goals sequenced in order of importance. By associating each task on her to-do list with one or more of these goals, she discovered which tasks added value and supported her desired future state. I watched as she gleefully marked tasks with comments like "forget about it," "delegate this," "finish ASAP," and (my personal favorite) "What was I thinking?"

Understanding and taking control of her innate desire to connect things to greater purpose offers a new filter through which to gauge priority and value. Her excitement in this discovery was a pleasure to witness.

Effective Communication
Communication is a required skill for any industry. All too often individuals forget the importance of sharing knowledge, providing status updates, or asking questions. The ability to communicate effectively is doubly essential in technology-based industries where instant messaging programs and team collaboration applications are the preferred form of interaction. One of my clients categorically refused to engage with members of the project team via any means other than face-to-face or phone conversations. He also studiously avoided video messaging and conference calls.

Consequently, his input frequently failed to enter the decision-making process and his ideas were overlooked. Discouraged and feeling small, he wanted to look for a new job. He hesitated to take this step, as he recognized these feelings and knew that most organizations employed technology to facilitate project communication. Instead, he reached out to a mutual acquaintance who put him in touch with me.

Very familiar with the communication requirements of software development projects, I quickly realized the need to identify the cause of his refusal to communicate via technology. From a strengths perspective, I remember being surprised to see the CliftonStrengths® talent of Communication® in his strongest talents. Individuals with dynamic communication talents tend to weave engaging stories and convey valuable messages using words. To find the disconnect, I needed more information.

After requesting and receiving permission from his manager, I joined the team's weekly status meeting and daily stand up calls as a silent observer. Watching him in action and witnessing how his team reacted to his comments provided the information necessary to craft my feedback. Long story short, his explanations were long-winded and jumped sporadically from topic to topic. Even if he found the desire (and the time) to update his ideas in the system, his messages would be so long I feared his teammates would ignore them. Just as they tuned him out whenever he spoke up during the face-to-face meetings. The issue was not necessarily his avoidance of technology. The problem was that his team viewed him as pretentious and overly talkative. One of his natural talents had become a point of weakness.

I knew that, no matter how carefully I chose my words, this feedback would be hard for him to hear. He remained silent for quite some time after I shared my observations. At one point, I think he almost left the room. Thankfully, he rallied and started asking questions. How do you know this? Can I fix this? What should I do? I answered the first two questions by elaborating on my observations and indicating that I believed the issue could be fixed. The third question I sidestepped by asking him to brainstorm potential next steps.

For the next hour, we listed a variety of different possibilities. I played devil's advocate and encouraged him to keep the ideas coming. Surprisingly, the idea that stuck involved components of the technology he disliked using word and character limitations. We settled on a method for developing his communication skills that required he limit the number of words used during each segment of conversation. In fact, he started using the collaboration application to practice. His teammates appreciated the effort, and he was astounded by the support they offered. A couple even elected to practice along with him.

Breaking the Barriers of Distrust

Another memorable coaching experience was when I worked with a Quality Assurance Manager who had received constructive feedback from a direct report regarding her leadership and decision-making abilities. The employee felt micro-managed and was frustrated with the constant changes in direction. The manager was similarly frustrated because this individual continuously questioned assignments and was not completing tasks. At this point, I had my suspicions about the specific talents in play but remained silent.

A couple of days later the manager's CliftonStrengths® results were in my Inbox. My suspicions were confirmed. The talent themes of Strategic® and Arranger® appeared dominant in her profile. After reviewing her Strengths Insight Report, I asked how others might interpret her talents. At first, she struggled to look beyond the positive traits of being able to "see the bigger picture" and the ability to "course correct in a dynamic environment." I dug deeper by asking about her feelings regarding change.

Her eyes lit up, and she spoke effusively about how much she loved change. How she relished the challenge of staying one step ahead of the game. Next, I asked her to consider what might happen if someone on her team did not share her appreciation for change. She then described, almost precisely, the frustrations outlined in the employee feedback. It took a second, but she grew silent as the realization sank in.

Once she recognized the existence of a potential disconnect, we started examining other possibilities beyond resistance to change. Armed with a mental list to be mindful of, she re-engaged with the employee. She learned that the cause of the misunderstanding was not fear of change. Instead, the resistance to change stemmed from an inability to see the purpose behind the constant shifts in priority and focus. The manager correctly interpreted the need for change, but she was not explaining the circumstances effectively. Her employee saw alterations for the sake of change and doubted her directives. This lack of trust diminished his productivity, which, in turn, intensified the manager's focus on micro-management. Helping this leader see herself in a new light allowed them to form a powerful team dynamic. Removing a blind spot in a leader's perspective and establishing a need for communication can break down the barriers of distrust and help everyone focus their energies on creating value for an organization.

Understanding is Key to Change

Identifying that one of a key leader's strongest talent themes was Context® turned out to be a game changer for one technology team. Seven team members were attempting to build relationships with potential clients and wanted to make changes to the procedure that would reduce the number of steps required to provide trial software functionality for evaluation. Their leader, who owned the process in question, refused to entertain any of the suggestions. Frustrated with the status quo, one of my clients, who is a member of the team, encouraged the leader to find out his talents and introduced him to me.

At this point, I was unaware of the frustrations felt by his team. The leader completed the assessment, and I helped him understand the basics of his talents. He was intrigued by the results. I could tell he was trying to connect with his talents. Unfortunately, the frustrations of the team members remained. The leader refused to entertain change.

My original client finally shared the specifics of the conflict with me. Together we approached the leader with the suggestion to explore the talents of the remaining six individuals and to look at the talents of the team holistically.

While conducting a pre-workshop survey of the goals and challenges facing the team, more than one person provided the feedback that the leader resisted change and cited the evaluation software scenario as an example. I proposed using this situation as part of a group exercise for the team. The leader was reluctant but finally agreed when I outlined the value of devising a viable solution for his team and their clients.

Individuals high in the CliftonStrengths® talent of Context® appreciate history and often look to the past to justify the future. When I reviewed the reports of the rest of the team members, I discovered that the leader's dominant strength was in their blind spot. They could not understand his need for historical data. They were unhappy and felt ill equipped to serve the clients efficiently. In the group exercise, we explored each step of the process in granular detail. We mind-mapped every nuance from the stakeholders involved to timelines to the rationale for each step of the procedure.

For the next 30 minutes, I moderated a debate on the pros and cons of each point with everyone wearing the "hat," or filter, of their top talent theme. During this conversation, the team members listened to the various perspectives and began to piece them together into unified solutions. I couldn't stop smiling when the analytically minded teammate took control of the conversation and started to logically connect the dots between options rooted in experience and future possibility. The team learned how to communicate their ideas effectively, and the leader learned that his team not only recognized but also appreciated his need for context. Soon after the session, they updated the procedure; however, the changes, which differed entirely from the original recommendations, were ideas born of collaboration rather than frustration.

Opening Doors

Through my affiliation with Toastmasters®, I met a young man eager to learn and move his way up the ladder in his organization. He always had a smile on his face and a warm greeting for everyone when he walked into the room. I watched as he delivered a hilarious speech to the club. The members present held their sides to contain their laughter, as tears poured down their faces. After the meeting, I caught up with him, and we talked about his reasons for joining the club.

I remember being speechless for a few minutes when he shared that he wanted to become a supervisor at his company but did not know how to tell management he was interested. He just stood confidently in front of an audience of at least 20 people, many of whom I knew to be senior leaders in their organizations, and kept their full attention for almost 10 minutes! The content he shared included clever anecdotes about co-worker interactions and calls received from customers. Clearly, he understood his role and had a firm grasp of the politics in his department.

I thought he would make a terrific team lead, and told him so. Unfortunately, he did not believe me.

Moved to help in any way I could, I offered to be his mentor in the club. For six months, I coached him in setting goals and practicing his speeches; however, we made no progress regarding his willingness to discuss opportunities with his leadership team. It was time for a more direct approach. One of the projects in the Toastmasters® competent communication manual requires speakers to research a topic and present their findings to the club. I proposed that he investigate how to get a promotion.

Two weeks later, he delivered another well-structured speech to the club. He shared detailed information regarding titles, role descriptions, credentials, and conversations with management. After the meeting, I overheard another club member ask him why he had not acted on his own advice. He claimed that the opportunity had yet to present itself.

The club member responded, "So what! Make it happen anyway." My mentee later told me that, at that moment, he finally understood what I had been trying to say to him. He also told me that I would make a great coach!

Ironically, I was just starting to entertain the idea of becoming a coach as these events unfolded. His feedback to me, which was exactly what I told him, was to "go for it." He even fed one of my well-worn statements back at me, "You don't know until you try." A few weeks later, he applied for and accepted a new role as a team leader. When he shared the excellent news with me, he told me to hurry up and get certified because he was going to need my help.

This happy go-lucky young man no longer hides behind humor to build his confidence. Understanding that he has a great deal to offer others cultivated a brilliant servant leadership mindset that he fully embraces. We recently introduced strengths-based coaching to our conversations, and he has become unstoppable in his desire to understand himself and his team members. His strongest CliftonStrengths® talents are Individualization® and Responsibility®. We spent a lot of time ensuring that he reserved enough energy for himself as he tailored assignments to improve the engagement levels of his team. He credits coaching for his success as a leader. The reality is that coaching opened a door in his mind. The rest was his strengths shining through.

Transcending Labels

Diving into the inner workings of your mind to examine talent and success allows you to identify and practice the skills that engage your soul. My strengths coach once tasked me with creating an "I am" statement for each of my strongest talents. I spent HOURS trying to select just the right words for these critical sentences. During this time, I explored my talent themes in detail, contemplated how I used my talents to achieve success and tried to view my actions from the perspective of different talent themes.

While evaluating my talents, I discovered ways to describe myself that transcend the labels society is fond of placing on us. For example, I am not merely a lifelong learner. I am an individual who lives and loves to learn because researching new subjects and problem-solving recharges my energy and enables me to flourish in dynamic and challenging environments. Reflecting on my talents changed my frame of reference and allowed me to see beyond generalized descriptors and into my unique self. In many ways, I felt like a fog had lifted from my mind. Energized and eager to learn more, I can only imagine the possibilities if the whole world experienced this type of clarity and inspiration firsthand.

The best part of exploring strengths is the realization that, especially in today's complex society, you are not expected to carry the weight of the world on your shoulders. Designing teams to include members who are passionate about different activities and possessing complementary talents inspire all involved. When individuals, couples, and groups act from a place of strength, they are happier, more focused, and confident. This confidence influences others in the office and the community.

The ripple effect of strengths empowerment is that it has the potential to be awe-inspiring. Imagine a society where everyone performs with passion. Teams where individuals comprehend their contribution to success and the creation of value. Organizations where collaboration cultivates trust and improves productivity. A world that embodies strength and embraces differences would be magical to behold.

ABOUT THE AUTHOR

Marcia Buzzella

Learner®, Achiever®, Relator®, Responsibility®, Significance®

Marcia Buzzella is a leadership consultant and Gallup-Certified Strengths Coach dedicated to using collaborative, authentic, purposeful inquiry to enhance the strengths, performance, and engagement of individuals and teams.

Using strengths-based approaches, she teaches how to achieve personal and team success by identifying shared objectives, talent development opportunities, and innovative tactics to encourage adoption of new concepts, tools, and methods of interaction.

Marcia also possesses a doctorate in business administration, with a specialization in leadership.

You can reach Marcia at:

Website: www.marciabuzzella.com
Email: MarciaBuzzella@gmail.com

Chapter 3 - Heidi Convery

....

FLOURISH THROUGH STRENGTHS

My first coaching sessions took place in my downstairs bathroom. (Feel free to re-read that statement, but you processed it correctly the first time.) I sat on the cold tile floor with my pen and notepad, my cell phone glued to my face with syrup, and children's music playing in the background. Some coaches may begin their careers in a quiet and inspiring home office or, perhaps in their workplace with encouragement from their employers. That, my friends, was not my journey. My "call to coach" made its presence known the year I stayed at home with my two children, who were then two and four years old. It was messy, exhausting, and chaotic. Nevertheless, the birthplace of purpose isn't always equipped with bleached floors and executive fountain pens.

Before my leap into CliftonStrengths® coaching, I served as a higher education administrator for several wonderful universities and colleges around the country. I conducted the hiring processes. I orchestrated the employee initiatives. In addition, I adjudicated student conduct hearings. My career was focused entirely on creating personal and professional growth opportunities for students and staff.

Talking it Out

The meat of my career took place between 2005 and 2016. I worked primarily with millennial students. Millennials often receive a heavy dose of criticism for several attributes of their generation, but one wonderful characteristic of theirs that I truly love is their need to talk it out. My exchanges with students would begin with "And how has your day been?" and end with, "Well, I think if you start the conversation with 'Mom, I want to move to the country and herd chickens,' she might not hear the rest of your plan." On paper, I was an administrator. In reality, I was a coach.

Our family moved from Tennessee to Texas for my husband's career, and once we were settled in our new home, I began my job search for university administration positions. The process was grueling. I adored my time in higher education, and continue to be blessed beyond measure by the students and staff that I worked alongside. But searching through university postings at that moment felt like I was sifting through wet cement. Everything looked the same. It felt heavy and lifeless. The longer I searched, the louder I could hear "This isn't it."

I kept thumbing through my mental filing cabinets. "Surely you've helped someone through something similar before? What advice did you give them?" Taking a note from my former millennial friends, I chose several close friends and family members to act as sounding boards while I "talked it out." Through the process, two consistencies surfaced: my love for coaching and my belief in the power of the CliftonStrengths® assessment. I knew I was at my best when helping others reach new levels of self-discovery; that was, after all, the reason I entered the field of higher education. But could I do this? Could I create my own coaching business in the midst of raising two toddlers and with only one income in our family? "Do it," whispered my Activator® talent. So I took a breath and jumped into the deep end.

While my love for coaching didn't present itself until well into my professional career, my infatuation with the CliftonStrengths®

assessment began a very long time ago. I was first introduced to the strengths movement as a senior at Texas Tech University. I was working in the Housing and Residential Life department as a Resident Assistant, and the organization provided the assessment to all of their student and professional staff. In all honesty, I didn't pay as much attention as I should have to the development exercises that our supervisors were providing. Graduation was less than a year away. I was applying to graduate schools across the country, and well, I was hugely distracted by my perceived priorities. But even through my inability to focus, I vividly remember reading my results. "Activator® – You make a decision, you take action, you look at the result, and you learn." Could that have been why I changed majors seven times in college? Is this why I never regretted all of the paperwork required, because I continued to learn from each decision? I was officially intrigued.

A Lens to Understanding Others

Several months later, I was accepted into the Higher Education graduate program at Florida Interntional University. As faith (or fate...but really, faith...) would have it, my assistantship was with the Housing and Residential Life department at the university. They just so happened to be incredibly involved with the growing strengths movement. My deep connection with strengths was cultivated here. Not only was I given the opportunity to gain a greater understanding of my own talents, but I learned the value of understanding the talents of those around me.

I transitioned from "Why does he always question everything I do in our meetings?," to "When he and I are finished with this project, it will be unstoppable because he's thought of every obstacle!" I didn't get to that mentality overnight, and in many ways I am still training my brain to use strengths as a lens through which to view others in a positive way. What I once found irritating in someone's behavior, I now saw as a valuable contribution. This is where my introduction to strengths application began.

Understanding your talents is incredibly beneficial and internally motivating, but being able to apply your knowledge to birth more proactive and productive decision-making is where the real magic happens. I will forever be grateful for that invaluable education. It laid the foundation for my future.

Self-Discovery and Talent Development

Great coaches have coaches. Some of the best coaches I've ever known spend significant time on their own personal and professional development. I knew a major factor in developing a successful business was for me to dive into my own talent growth. Specifically, what talents of mine could be incredibly helpful when beginning my entrepreneurial journey? Could any of them potentially cause me a headache or two? I had a lot of anxiety around the nuts and bolts of creating my coaching company. How do I build a website? Where do I begin with my marketing? How do I present myself as legitimate in this vast world of coaching? UGH. I needed to find clarity and the world's largest cup of coffee. Let's add a piece of coffee cake in there, too.

I sought the help of a seasoned strengths coach during the formation of my business. He and I broke down my apprehension into digestible pieces and began applying my strengths to those obstacles. For example, I knew one of my first accomplishments needed to be establishing an online presence. Producing an appealing, navigational website is a non-negotiable pillar of a successful business today. I could feel a particular talent hindering my productivity. "If your website doesn't appear professional and established, no one will take your coaching seriously," taunted my Significance® talent.

A new concept that my coach recommended was to personify my talents and allow them to "speak" to one another. What would my Learner® say to my Significance® in this moment? How would my Maximizer® approach this situation differently? They began to "argue" with one another and suddenly, I could see new possibilities.

And just like that, my approach began to change. I discovered that the moments that cause me stress and anxiety are typically those when I am too focused on what needs to happen, and have forgotten that my strengths lie in the present. The result of this kind of conversation is that it paves the way to discover the unknown and to begin to use our own talents to solve problems independently. Our strengths are our real-life superpowers.

Cultivating Strengths

One of my first, and favorite, coaching relationships was with Rebekah, an operations manager at a small financial planning firm. The bulk of her responsibilities included managing the operations and administrative staff of the business, as well as responding to unplanned fires throughout the workday. Rebekah came to me for two reasons: she was struggling to motivate and engage her employees, and she was experiencing a complete lack of motivation in her role. Those were two pretty huge boulders, but both were solvable problems by deliberating on two questions: 1) Who am I? and 2) Who am I as a manager? I know that sounds incredibly vague, but the tangible, specific action items that come from successful coaching all begin with questions similar to these.

When I first met with Rebekah, her CliftonStrengths® knowledge was very common. She had taken the assessment a few years back, read the report, found it amusing, and then moved on. When I saw her talent profile, I could see a potential reason for part of her motivational collapse at work, so that's where our conversation began. I asked Rebekah how often she had the opportunity to perfect processes in her position. "Never," she answered. "I'm always trying to solve unexpected fires quickly, so I don't have the time to make our procedures better. They work, I guess, but they aren't where they could be, and that's frustrating for me."

Although her Arranger® talent was able to quickly assess problems and organize the pieces to seek resolution, her Maximizer® talent was not being engaged AT ALL. She was missing that ability to achieve excellence, and instead, felt as if she had to settle for the status quo. We began to search for ways Rebekah could more intentionally engage her Maximizer® talent in her role. "Have you ever kept a small list of the problems that arise to see if any consistencies exist? What problems tend to repeat themselves?" Rebekah stared off into space, and you could almost hear the hamster climb aboard the wheel.

If she could identify consistent problems, perhaps a procedure could use some tweaking to prevent further issues and improve the business operations. I could see her Maximizer® leap for the door! She couldn't wait to get back to the office and start searching for ways to engage her natural talent of taking good to great. Fixing small procedural issues meant less future workday fires, which meant more time to tweak additional processes. We were cultivating her strengths and creating her dream job.

Regarding Rebekah's employee engagement challenges, we also spoke at great length about the talents of her employees. Could her people be experiencing a similar dissatisfaction as she had in her position? Rebekah supervised several of her team members dominant in the CliftonStrengths® talent of Belief®. I asked Rebekah about ways she could help those employees feel connected to the purpose and values of the organization. I suggested they might be missing the bigger picture. "You know what? One of my employees just recently asked if our business ever got involved with community service projects. I didn't make the connection then, but maybe she's trying to find a bigger purpose in what we do?" YES! We brainstormed ways Rebekah could coordinate philanthropic opportunities in her organization. This was the very tip of the iceberg.

Rebekah and I continued to spend time together over the next several months discussing ways she could actively engage her strengths in her position and how she could help her employees do the same. The possibilities for purposeful success are endless, and in the business setting, it begins with the manager.

Creating Team Culture

I love the depth I can reach within individual coaching sessions, but I feel as though coaching managers and teams can have an incredibly profound impact. Only one-third of employees in the U.S. are engaged in their jobs, according to statistics. ONE-THIRD. My sense of urgency to help managers learn to engage and empower their team is significant, and one of the greatest experiences I've had doing just that was with a small tech business.

The leadership of this small technology company came to me looking to build a positive, familial culture within their organization. They were looking to create an entire culture of engagement. Like many other technology companies, some of the employees held positions that didn't necessarily require them to interact with others on a consistent basis. They were mostly self-sufficient in set-up and only collaborated with small groups as needed. As you can imagine, office birthday celebrations were awkward.

I began my work with the managers because I ALWAYS start with the managers. Did you know that studies show that 70% of the variance in workplace culture is dependent upon the manager? That's an enormous amount of responsibility! Managers who are now feeling a little uncomfortable, keep reading.

The management team had varying levels of leadership experience, and they had all worked in the technology field for the vast majority of their careers. My first meeting with the team was spent asking questions about their people. What were they wanting to see happen in the organization? Why was developing a culture vital to them? I also discussed the CliftonStrengths® assessment and how important understanding the strengths of your employees is when building engagement and empowering culture. "Won't that assessment be a little pointless," one of the managers laughed. "I mean, we are all in tech. We think the same way. You're probably only going to find a bunch of analytical, numbers-loving results." And just as quickly as the words left his mouth, it was incredibly clear as to why culture and engagement didn't exist in the company.

Thankfully, I was able to communicate how important knowing employees' strengths would be to group development, so we proceeded to administer the assessment. I STILL remember the meeting with those five managers when I delivered a chart listing all of their employees' talents. Not only were Strategic Thinking themes not dominant in the organization, they were dead last compared to the other three categories of strengths (Rath & Conchie, Strengths Based Leadership: Great Leaders, Teams, and Why People Follow, 2008). We were all astounded! And the most common talent theme among the group? Relator®. OF COURSE engagement was an issue! People with a dominant Relator® strength crave deeper relationships with others. It doesn't mean they want to be on an incredibly vulnerable level with every single person in their cubicle range, but certainly with a select few. I observed that the managers were not encouraging deeper connections between colleagues. It was an organization of walls.

We spent the next several months working on initiatives that would allow employees to connect with one another. The management team began to host "Get to Know…" weekly events, which highlighted a different CliftonStrengths® talent theme each week. The events were organized to allow small groups to form and encourage deeper and more transparent conversations. The change in employee engagement was revolutionary, and the addition of intentional workplace culture initiatives was transformative. This wasn't a client relationship that ended after one group development session. We had significant work to do, and my involvement with the organization lasted several months. Because we started this cultural shift with the management team, the positive momentum has done nothing but gain speed.

The leaders are now leading the change, not the coach. The leaders became the coaches. In my opinion, the objective of any coaching relationship should be to empower the management team to coach their own people to success.

Transforming Significant Relationships

Occasionally I will coach couples who want to better their relationship by understanding one another's strengths. Honestly, I think it should be mandatory for couples entering committed relationships or marriages because it can provide you with an incredible communication platform. The biggest source of positive feedback I receive from clients is "Now we have words for what we've 'known' about one another all along! And they aren't four-letter words!"

One of my most impactful discoveries came from my own relationship. My husband, Mark, is dominant in the talent theme Deliberative®. He spends much of his time assessing risk before making decisions. It's important to him that the decision he makes is as safe and accurate as possible. In contrast, I am strong in the talent theme Activator®. I jump. I believe learning will take place in the moment, so I typically don't spend time researching or deliberating. We process at opposite ends of the spectrum.

My favorite example of our polarity occurred shortly after we were married. I remember the moment so distinctly. Mark and I were watching TV one night when he announced, "I think we need to buy a new TV."

"Great!" I said, and though it was 9 pm, I got up to get my shoes and bag. "What are you doing?" he asked with a sincerely confused look on his face.

"You said we needed a new TV, so I was getting my shoes on to get ready to go." It made perfect sense to me.

"Babe, you can't just go out and buy a TV without researching it. What are you going to do, just walk in and pick one?" he asked. "I mean...yeah?" I said, hugely confused.

I took my shoes off and sat down, guessing he would hop on his laptop to do his research. Then, maybe we could go pick out a TV the next day after work? Well, that's not what happened! Three months passed. Three months later, we went and purchased our new TV. I was in complete agony for three months knowing that a decision needed to be made and we weren't making it. But when we went into the store, the look of assuredness that Mark had on his face was remarkable. He knew precisely what TV to get and it was in that moment that I recognized how different we were. And I was so thankful that he had deliberated so thoroughly and we were purchasing the right television for us. I learned I could lean on that strength of his when I knew we had a decision to make in our marriage that might be costly or highly impactful.

And from Mark's perspective, he will tell you that my Activator® talent is responsible for so many wonderful, spontaneous moments in our life together. He's been delighted by random drives to the middle of nowhere, packing up and moving across the country, and spelunking into 11-inch rock spaces. I give him spontaneity, and he keeps me grounded. Don't get me wrong; we have to work on understanding one another's talents on a daily basis. But we've grown to understand the importance of what those strengths bring to the balance of our relationship.

Greatness Is Not Reserved for a Few
Coaching others has been a life-changing experience. It has changed my life and my family's lives in many ways. People are incredible. I often leave a coaching session saying, "Man, that was a cool person!" What a dull and limiting place we would find ourselves in without differentiating thought.

I deeply appreciate the variety of strengths coaching experiences I'm able to have with clients. There's such a variety in the way we problem solve, innovate, collaborate and relate to others. The odds of someone matching your list of 34 Strengths in the same order is 1 in 474 billion. There's not another person on this planet that thinks like you (Rath, *StrengthsFinder 2.0*, 2007).

The strengths philosophy isn't meant to be a skin-deep experience. Understanding the way we think, interact with others, and process our surroundings is so vital to building strong, healthy relationships, whether that be managerial, team, or intimate. We have each been given such an incredibly unique set of gifts to use for others and ourselves. Greatness isn't reserved for a few. It's achieved when we understand our talents and begin putting them in situations to excel. We have a world full of need and now is the perfect time to put all of our strengths to work.

About the Author

Heidi Convery
Activator®, Learner®, Input®, Belief®, Includer®

Heidi Convery is the founder and owner of Flourish LLC, an organization dedicated to the engagement and development of managers and teams. Through individual coaching sessions and professional development seminars, Heidi uses a personal and interactive approach to help her clients identify their challenges, and learn to apply their strengths for the greatest productivity, profitability and progress.

Heidi is a Gallup-Certified Strengths Coach and holds a Master's Degree in Higher Education Administration.

You can reach Heidi at:

Website: www.begintoflourish.com
Email: heidi@begintoflourish.com

Chapter Four - Alicia Santamaria

....

FINDING FORWARD

Have you ever had even a fleeting aspiration or longing to pursue a different career or life path at some vague, ambiguous, later point in your life? Perhaps it is an impractical ambition or possibly a complete departure from your current trajectory that might involve stepping outside of your comfort zone and taking a risk?

I have. And the first big questions to myself were always: "How do I know when it is time?" "When does the future become the present?"

My next big questions were; "What does it take to set aside self-limiting beliefs and dispel any doubts?" "How can I channel the very best of my talents, skills, and strengths so I cannot fail in making it happen?"

It was in 2010 when "later" became "now" with the help of a friend who knew about my aspirations to quit full-time employment and become a self-employed consultant. Someday. When I was "older." I had this notion that to be a successful, self-employed consultant, I needed to be more seasoned, needed more experience under my belt. My 40th birthday was coming up the following year and this friend very thoughtfully and with a hint of sarcasm finally said to me, "You might be old enough now, you know." The future had become the present. The time was now to find my forward.

Since I wasn't satisfied or feeling valued in my job any longer, it seemed like as good a time as any to leap. Not quite a mid-life crisis, getting close to age 40 did put things into perspective for me. I told myself that if I couldn't make it work, I could always find another job but if I didn't try, I would have regrets. So, with my family's support, serious financial consideration, and a lot of positive self-talk, I began to sketch out my roadmap. I knew I needed to figure out what I had to offer that would differentiate me in a vast sea of consultants. Why would anyone want to hire me? Over the course of my professional career, I had gained many years of experience as a mediator, group facilitator, and conflict resolution/communication skills trainer. Combined with my Master's Degree in Interpersonal and Intercultural Communication, it seemed a pretty firm foundation on which to build my services and offerings. After further reflection, however, I decided that I needed something more. Leaning into my own transformational experiences with a coach, I set my sights on adding coaching to my tool belt.

After talking to other coaches and researching my options, I selected a program in nearby San Rafael, California, called The Coaches Training Institute. As I was going through the coach training program, I voraciously read and studied current trends in personal and organizational learning and development to augment my professional experience. I remember one day in particular spending hours at my local Barnes & Noble bookstore. I must have looked through about 20 books that afternoon, but the one that jumped off the shelf at me was a small red and white hardback book called StrengthsFinder 2.0 by Tom Rath. Inside was a code to take an online talent assessment from the Gallup Corporation. As a lifelong learner and one always interested in further self-development, it was right up my alley. When I got home with it, I quickly cut open the small envelope in the back of the book to access the code and eagerly got online to take the assessment.

My Lightbulb Moment

In about 40 minutes, I had in my hands a report that named my strongest talents. I quickly learned that what the assessment measures are natural talents. These talents are our greatest potential for strength with the investment of skills and knowledge. As an approach to development, focusing on your strengths and using them to manage your weakness will yield greater performance and success.

After reading the book and my assessment results, I experienced a lightbulb moment that has stayed with me to this day. I suddenly understood myself in a new way. It was a pivotal moment in my personal development, just as I was about to embark on a journey towards helping others with their development. Not always one for having good timing, this was impeccable.

So, what was this lightbulb moment exactly? The talent that rose to the absolute top for me, that had the highest intensity based on my responses on the assessment, was Communication®. I did a double take when I first read it. "What?" I asked myself (probably out loud, knowing me). You mean to say that this thing about me, this thing that I have disliked about myself, gotten in trouble for, and tried to change about myself my whole life, is something good? It was as if the world shifted under my feet as I started to let myself imagine what it would mean for me if the very thing I had spent the last 20 years of my life trying to fix was actually my greatest source of power.

You see, I am a member of the tribe of talkers. You know who they are. Those people who have to process experiences, emotions, ideas, and events out loud. Those people who brought home report cards from elementary school through high school that said, "good student, but talks too much in class." Those people who enjoy explaining, re-explaining experiences, telling, retelling stories, and then embellishing some more.

Maybe you are one of these people and have Communication® high on your list of talents, too. If so, you probably can understand what it is like to feel like you can't control your mouth sometimes and want to kick yourself for opening it one too many times in a meeting or a meaningful conversation. My assessment results illuminated that this talent is something great about me, not a weakness that needs fixing.

It is a small but crucial shift. Although I must take great care to not overuse my gift of gab, if I invest my efforts intentionally, that is where my highest potential for excellence lies. The strengths approach isn't about ignoring weaknesses or pigeonholing people. The capacity for development when you start with natural talent is limitless.

The Power of Naming

My experience of learning and studying my other strongest talents was as rewarding, though it manifested differently. With my Communication® talent, the very word had instant and deep meaning for me. Aside from something I had gotten in trouble for at various times in my life, being an open and honest communicator was something on which I prided myself. It held tremendous value for me.

I remember working for someone early on in my career who was a very opaque communicator. She would only tell you what she thought you needed to know. I often felt challenged by this lack of transparency and found it very difficult to be successful in a workplace culture that did not value direct and honest communication and dialogue. Our greatest strengths often shape our values and for me, communication is at the core of who I am.

My other top talents, however, were not necessarily ones that I could have named the way my CliftonStrengths® report did. There is tremendous power in naming something that exists as previously unidentified. Naming something helps to define it and bring it into our sphere of knowledge. For example, another one of my top talents is Individualization®. Is that even a word? However, once I understood what it meant, I got over my initial skepticism. And as I began to unpack what each of the talent words represented, the light bulb shone even brighter. My talents were illuminated in new ways! I was finally connected to my unique genius. Psychologist Donald O. Clifton, who developed the CliftonStrengths® assessment noted: "We live with them every day, and they come so easily to us that they cease to be precious (Buckingham & Clifton, 2001)."

The Process of Becoming

As I continued with my coaching training and certification, planned the exit from my job, and created my business plan, I dove deeper and deeper into the world of strengths development. Although I had started with my own results, I found myself fascinated by others' experience with their results and the implications for how this could benefit teams. I think many of us not only take our talents and strengths for granted but also wonder why people are not more like us. I wanted to learn more about this process of uncovering and giving voice to our unique combination of talents.

I continued to read and study more from the body of fields of positive psychology and organizational development research. While I uncovered a deep and robust understanding of my unique strengths, I started applying it directly to the task before me, then starting my consulting and coaching business. By this time, I knew coaching was going to be an important a part of my service offerings, in addition to training and facilitation. I knew that I wanted to coach individuals and teams using the strengths development methodology. Coaching became a mission.

Let Your Life Speak author Parker Palmer writes, "What a long time it can take to become the person one has always been (Palmer, 2015)." Eight years after I started this journey, I am now a proud Professional Certified Coach as accredited by the International Coach Federation, a Gallup-Certified Strengths Coach, and the successful CEO of my own consulting business. I have done all this by leveraging my talents as strengths in a way I never imagined was possible.

Like an alchemist, I have learned how to combine my strengths in different ways to give my clients my best, while working to bring out the best in them. I have an insatiable desire to learn, combined with my need to gather, consume, and dispense resources and information that gives a client just the tools they need. I'm able to connect quickly with people and see them as the unique individuals they are. This connection enables a client to trust me and want to work together. I bring energy and warmth to a room as I share knowledge and skills that engages and resonates with the audience. I customize my approach and my services to meet clients where they are. I continually stay on top of the latest trends in organizational and personal development. After more than 20 years of being in the workforce, I finally feel like I am doing exactly what I was meant to be doing.

The Right Key for the Right Lock

Can you imagine how frustrating it is to try to unlock a door when you don't have the right key? And what if you don't realize that it's the wrong key, and you repeatedly try to jam the mismatched key into the lock?

It is this unconscious autopilot state we can get into when we aren't paying enough attention to what is in front of us, and we convince ourselves of what the truth must be. I see that happening with people who are on a developmental journey. Maybe they are trying to get better at something or change a habit. Unless they are using the right key, it isn't going to open the lock.

One of the most rewarding aspects of being a strengths coach is helping people achieve higher performance and goal attainment by using strategies customized for who they are based on their strengths. It helps people find the right key for their lock.

For example, if you are a task-oriented, get-it-done person with the CliftonStrengths® talent of Achiever®, your orientation to work will more often than not take precedence over relationships. You might get feedback from your supervisor that you need to be more "relational" or hear complaints from your friends that they never see you because you are always working. Trying to force you to stop working magically is not a strengths-based approach to your development. Instead, since you love to-do lists and are naturally inclined to want to get things checked off, why not try including an item like "call three friends this week" or "include icebreaker in meeting with the full team." If I am your friend, trust me, I don't care if you are calling me because it was on your to-do list. I will be thrilled to hear from you!

One of my clients, Lucia, sought coaching "to improve her leadership presence, her people skills in dealing with different personalities and work styles, and become a better communicator that presents more gracefully." She had worked in the construction industry for almost 20 years before coming to her present job in a more professional working environment. After receiving a promotion and straightening out some staff issues, she decided it was time to focus on her development in this different work environment.

I recall one particular coaching conversation where we explored her desire to improve her presentation skills. Although she felt she did an okay job, with Communication® as one of her strongest talents, she wanted to do better. She shared that there were times when she felt awkward, nervous, and self-conscious when she presented to a group, mainly depending on who was in the audience. As she envisioned how she would like to feel when speaking and what would be different, it became clear that she might do better with a more interactional style of presenting. She said she hated just giving all this information out and not knowing if people were getting it or understanding her. We brainstormed some ideas of how she could make it more interactive and conversational rather than a lecture. She also thought it would be helpful to give herself some positive self-talk as she was heading into a presentation. What Lucia did not need was a typical approach to improving public speaking. It was leveraging her Communication® strength in different ways that provided the right key for her.

As another example, I was coaching Carlos, a mid-level manager whose supervisor had identified some areas of development in which she wanted him to focus. When the three of us met to set the goals of the coaching session, she shared that there were times she needed Carlos to be more quick and nimble and to be able to make decisions without always having a backup plan. She told him, "Sometimes I just need you to be able to jump with me even if we don't know exactly where we will land." For Carlos, this was like asking a fish to fly! Even though Carlos had Achiever® as a top strength, it was because of his high Deliberative® and Responsibility® talents that he was cautious and risk averse. To help find the right key to unlock his developmental opportunity, I encouraged him to try to identify what he would need to enable him to jump with her rather than resist. He replied, "I would need to know how high the cliff is." As we explored the metaphor further, they agreed that she would do more to lay out the risks as well as the need for urgency in those situations when his cautiousness could have been a barrier. We reframed what being "responsible" looked like in these situations and tapped into his high need for productivity to get him "doing" at the pace the work demanded from them.

Sometimes finding the right key for the right lock in strengths coaching comes from a deep examination of the ways our talents influence each other. Sean, a successful senior leader in a large technology organization, was using coaching to help him improve his people management skills. As he put it, "I struggle with the fluffy stuff." Getting his CliftonStrengths® results helped him understand that his high Empathy® and Relator® talents serve to complement his more introverted Intellection®, Learner®, and Deliberative® strengths. It was because of his intuitive sense of others' emotional states that kept his door open for people if they needed to talk. That sounded pretty "fluffy" to me, but the challenge for him came when people moved beyond talking about work-related issues. He identified how uncomfortable he would get if someone shared something they were stressed about at home or about a personal challenge they were facing. This was what he meant by "fluffy stuff."

Because of his relational talents, he was self-critical of his discomfort and hesitancy in doing more for his direct reports and colleagues in conversations that weren't just strictly about work problems. As we talked more about his unease, he discovered that it was coming from his sense that if someone shared something personal with him, he was expected to reciprocate. He was very clear that he was not comfortable sharing his personal stories at work, a hallmark of his high Deliberative® strength. He realized he could be more understanding with other people sharing and disclosing as long as they didn't expect it from him.

This realization helped us find the right key for this particular area of development. Instead of reciprocating or feeling as if he had to share something personal of his own, he would respond using active listening skills to reflect back to people so they felt heard. Sean was already a great listener, so this wasn't difficult. It is in this way that Sean recognized the impact of one strength on another and is now truly making the most of his Relationship Building talent themes (Rath & Conchie, *Strengths Based Leadership: Great Leaders, Teams, and Why People Follow*, 2008).

Not Just Like Us

The strengths approach to development helps us to recognize that our combination of talents is what leads us to our highest levels of performance. What makes us unique also makes us different, though not more or less than others. In the workplace, these differences influence and impact our relationships, the ability to get work done, decision-making, team dynamics, and just about everything. The fact is that people are not exactly like us and even though we know this cognitively, we somehow have these moments of amnesia that lead us to feel frustrated and misunderstood when someone doesn't do or say something like we would.

We forget that people are not just like us when we are trying to complete a project and the person we need to finish a critical piece is out of the office that day. "How could they be so irresponsible?" we ask.

We forget that people are not just like us when we are told to make an important decision without all the data and facts we need. "How can they possibly expect me to move forward with such little information?" we ask.

We forget that people are not just like us when a supervisor focuses on all the things that went wrong with a client project and wants to know how we'll fix it for next time. "Why can't she ever focus on the positive and what goes well in our meetings?" we ask.

We forget that people are not just like us when a colleague doesn't say anything during an important meeting but days later shares insights that are brilliant. "Why couldn't he have come up with those brilliant ideas during the meeting when it mattered?" we ask.

One of the most dramatic transformations I have seen people make as a result of strengths-based coaching is when they learn how to view things from other people's perspective and to appreciate the value of those differences. As I continued to work with Lucia beyond improving her presentation style, it has been amazing to see the transformation she has had around her goal to learn how to work with different styles in better ways. She came into coaching with very clear ideas of how other people should behave based on her own set of strengths. She would get impatient and judgmental when others didn't say or do something the way she thought they should. She would say things like "I don't get it. Why can't he just...? That's how I would do it."

Fortunately, Lucia has Learner® as one of her top strengths. She has been open to feedback from me when reminded that not everyone is like her! Over the past nine months of working together, she has learned how to look at things from others' perspectives. Anaïs Nin once wrote: "We do not see things as they are. We see things as we are." Lucia has come to understand the bias that comes from her strengths perspective and how to be more empathetic with others. Her transformation became evident to me when she recounted a recent conversation with her supervisor.

She was preparing to have a difficult conversation with a direct report she had been struggling with for many months. She asked her supervisor if she would role-play the conversation with her before actually talking to the employee. Lucia asked her supervisor to play the employee, and she practiced trying to be more open and empathetic. As Lucia recounted to me later, "my boss almost fell out of her chair after our roleplay. She said that coaching with you had been the best money we ever spent!" After I wiped the happy grin off my face and congratulated her, I asked her what she had said and done in the role-play that was such an improvement in the eyes of her supervisor. She replied, "I asked questions, instead of following my normal instinct which is to tell that person exactly what I think and what they did wrong." She was able to shift her perspective of this employee and recognize her value. Lucia's supervisor knows her to be a direct and blunt person and that she was working to soften herself and be more flexible in working with different styles and personalities, especially those who were more sensitive. Her feedback to Lucia was a testament to her transformation.

Later, when Lucia held the conversation with her employee, she was able to show empathy instead of immediate disapproval when the employee tried to blame others. Lucia used active listening, responded to the employee "I can understand how you can feel overwhelmed with the amount of work…", and then went on to ask open-ended questions. She told me about several other "intentional moments" when she caught herself from reacting negatively and instead sought to be empathetic. I asked her what she thought the impact on the employee was by her responding this way and she said, "That she feels like I do care, even if I am not verbally empathetic." Lucia even kept her Achiever® talent in check and gave the employee an additional week to meet the deadline.

That was something else we had been working on. Her high Achiever® and Responsibility® strengths give her incredible stamina and the instinct to take on more than she probably should. It can be tough to work for someone with these strengths if you don't have them. Lucia has done a lot to recognize that most people can't keep up with her and that she has to be intentional about ensuring her work/life balance. Her next step is to have her team take the CliftonStrengths® assessment so she can do more to understand their uniqueness while they learn more about her. A robust team-building tool helps managers be better managers and allows colleagues to work together in new and more productive ways.

A Common Language
In addition to having the privilege of accompanying extraordinary individuals on their strengths journeys, I also love working with teams. Strengths-based development is an approach that helps team members identify how they can purposely aim their talents so that the team is better equipped to accomplish its goals and performance objectives and respond to everyday situations. Team members work more productively together and are more successful at reaching their goals when they recognize and value their colleagues' strengths and know how to effectively partner together.

Many of the teams I work with report that participating in team strengths learning sessions provides them with a universal language that helps increase the quality of their conversations and dialogue with one another.

I recall my experience working with the leadership team of a small start-up company who found that learning about each other's strengths gave them insight and a new understanding of how they could better partner with each other to take the company to the next level. They recognized why they sometimes had conflict and identified when their intentions and their impact didn't line up.

They were able to forgive each other more readily when they didn't see eye to eye on something and put forth more effort to understand the other person's perspective. A renewed focus on partnership enabled them to identify where they could complement and augment each other's strengths in ways that are more powerful. Putting aside ego and the notion they each needed to be good at everything, they could settle into their strength niches and serve the team and company in ways that are more productive.

As much as strengths development can enhance a team's cohesiveness and productivity, it is even more potent if the entire organization embraces a strengths approach. An organizational investment can lead to an increase in employee engagement and a more positive work environment. As I look ahead to the future of my coaching and where

I hope the strengths movement is heading, it is towards depth. It is great to have more than 18 million people around the world knowing their strengths but how can we leverage that to go beyond individual development?

Whenever I get brought in to coach a team, I work hard to help them find ways to leverage their investment and embed strengths into their culture. My most significant challenge is when a team building exercise on strengths is a one-time event. There is so much an organization can benefit from when leaders successfully leverage their strengths, managers coach and bring out the best in their teams, and employees are engaged in doing what they do best every day.

Strengths development has tremendous potential to make a difference in our workplaces and organizations. But what if our families, communities, cities, and even countries were also able to leverage the power of strengths fully? I genuinely believe it would transform the world.

About the Author

Alicia Santamaria

Communication®, Individualization®, Woo®, Learner®, Input®

As CEO of adelante coaching + consulting, Alicia delivers dynamic learning and development coaching and organizational consulting to facilitate people, teams, and organizations forward. A Gallup-Certified Strengths Coach, Alicia guides clients in deepening their understanding of their natural talents and transforming them into high performing strengths. She partners with organizational leaders and people managers to collaboratively design and implement individualized strengths-based programs to meet their team development goals.

Alicia incorporates her background in conflict resolution in her use of the CliftonStrengths® tool to help teams increase their understanding of each other, leverage differences, and improve the quality of their communication.

You can reach Alicia at:

Website: www.adelantecc.com
Email: alicia@adelantecc.com
LinkedIn: www.linkedin.com/in/aliciasantamaria

Chapter Five - David G. Boop, Ed. D.

CAREER COACHING IN THE TWENTY-FIRST CENTURY

After college, I went home having earned a History degree from the College of Wooster in Ohio. Like many college graduates before me, I had no idea what I wanted to do with my degree. My hometown of Bloomsburg, Pennsylvania, is home to a state university. My father arranged for me to visit with the director of the career center at the university to discuss my career options. During our conversation, I recall asking the director, "How do you get a job in career planning?" and he proceeded to talk with me. My fascination with long-term personal success in careers began.

While I temporarily tabled my interest in working for a collegiate career center, my first job with the Boy Scouts of America only increased my interest in personal career success. I worked in the division of Scouting called Exploring, which helps young adults discover career opportunities. My main function as the Exploring Executive was to encourage community-based organizations to sponsor an Explorer Post, which in turn provided young adults a chance to gain valuable insights into vocational options. After a few years of working with the Boy Scouts, I returned home to central Pennsylvania to work for a regional economic development organization. While I enjoyed my five years working in economic development, I could never forget my conversation with the career center director. I wanted to work in a collegiate career center. Thus, it was back to college to pursue my first graduate degree, a Master's of Arts in Student Affairs in Higher Education.

Over the next two decades, I spent most of my time working in academic career development centers in Georgia, North Carolina, Arkansas, and Indiana. At my last three stops, I was the director of a college or university career center. However, I was acutely aware that the career journey for Baby Boomers and subsequent generations would be far different than that of the Silent Generation and previous generations. In short, people born after World War II would encounter a more fluid job market which would require frequent job and career moves. My conscience started to gnaw at me. If the marketplace required numerous job changes, how do traditional career center services like resume critiques and mock interviews help people navigate their career success in the twenty-first century?

My Own Strengths Journey

My strengths journey began in the spring of 1997. I attended a conference of the two largest student affairs professional associations in Chicago, Illinois. During the conference, there was one break-out workshop sponsored by the University of Washington that I found particularly interesting. I wasn't the only one interested in the session. There was a standing-room only crowd for the presentation! The session concentrated on the use of the Dependable Strengths Articulation Process with University of Washington alumni. DSAP is a series of exercises that create discussion opportunities in small groups. You discover the stories of your life and get feedback about what makes you unique. You identify and prove strengths through a discussion process that is interactive, improves self-esteem, and increases motivation. I became a believer in strengths development during this presentation.

In January of 1999, I became the Director of the Career Center at Lenoir-Rhyne University in North Carolina. The idea of incorporating strengths development into my knowledge base had not diminished in the subsequent two years since the DSAP presentation by the University of Washington staff. Fortunately, the Director of the Alumni Office at my new post wanted to assist alumni who were increasingly searching out services to help them change jobs or careers. Soon after, I was able to receive funding to attend a five-day training in Seattle to become a Dependable Strengths Facilitator. I was one of about twenty participants attending the training session. While the entire training was a paradigm shift in my way of thinking about human development and long-term career success, I was especially impacted by six members of the group from South Africa who were attending the training to help congregants in their church to obtain employment. The training reinforced my belief in the strengths development movement. Upon my return from Seattle, I facilitated a successful group session for ten of our alumni. The success of the group session planted a seed in my mind to spend more time doing what I love; to help people drive their careers forward through the understanding of their unique excellence.

After completing my doctorate in Higher Education from the University of Georgia, I accepted a job as the Director of Career Services at Arkansas Tech University. Shortly after I started at the school, my supervisor made me aware of the CliftonStrengths® assessment. As you might imagine, I was quite interested in the tool and Gallup's higher education initiatives. Fortunately, my supervisor encouraged me to attend a CliftonStrengths® for Students Instructor training in the fall of 2008. I flew to Minneapolis in December to complete the training and upon my return, I facilitated a few great training sessions. I knew that a focus on strengths was key and I had a longing to devote more time in that area. Unfortunately, I was not in a position to expand my strengths development efforts.

The one thing I recall succinctly was my reaction to my own CliftonStrengths® results. Through a quick glance at Gallup's Strengths Insight Guide, I was able to see and claim some of my talents. I immediately embraced Context® as a top talent. I have always been drawn to understand historical events and people. Not surprisingly, I was a history major in college and have a Bachelor's Degree in History!

I also clearly identified with Responsibility® as a talent of mine. I have always taken pride in my ability to complete what I start. My friends rely on my punctuality and follow-through. As I gained more understanding, I also knew that this was the one talent that exasperated me, especially at times when I would take ownership for things outside of my control. As I would learn later, there are shadow sides of strengths when they are misapplied.

In the early 1990's, I learned about the Johari Window, a tool created by two American psychologists, Joseph Luft and Harrington Ingham, in 1955. It is a technique used to help people better understand their relationship with themselves as well as others. The window is divided into four quadrants, which are labelled Open, Hidden, Blind, and Unknown. The Blind section indicates information not known to self but known to others. The Unknown section indicates information that is not known to self or others. I believe the power of the CliftonStrengths® assessment is to provide people with information that may be unknown to them. The tool has helped me understand my "superpowers" and how I can intentionally discuss the ways I can best contribute to everything I do.

For example, I've often described myself as an introverted and introspective person. As you might imagine, I've never considered myself capable of networking with people in social environments. However, I have discovered over a period of years my most natural way to get to know other people. I began to understand that my talent theme of Individualization® prompted me to want to understand the unique talents of others. My results helped me understand why I wanted to have meaningful conversations with other people to get to know them better.

As I began to comprehend how my top talents interacted with one another, I started to see how my Context® talent could complement my Individualization® as the most natural way to network with new people. I now understand that when I meet new people, I instinctively look for ways in which my previous life experiences intersect with the life experiences of the other person. It usually doesn't take me long to find something in common with those I meet. This revelation has helped me become a better networker.

Everyone Needs a Coach

As I shared previously, my desire to transition from working in a collegiate career center to a full-time strengths coach began out of frustration. It took me two decades to figure out that advising people is much less effective than coaching people. Too often, the students and alumni I advised were simply looking for pointers to make their resumes more impactful or tips on how to impress potential employers during an interview. I longed to interact in a transformational way with clients to help them with long-term career success.

It was frustrating to me that I was merely providing them with guidance they may or may not heed. But the times I worked with a client for five or six times, I witnessed their recognition of their distinctive accomplishments as they felt more confident to undertake a twenty-first century job search. Through trial and error, I began to understand that coaching people worked in almost every situation, while advising folks garnered positive outcomes irregularly.

At the first CliftonStrengths® Summit in July of 2016, Gallup® unveiled a new motto: Everyone Needs a Coach. The concept of a coach who can provide timely and meaningful feedback to improve performance has long been accepted in athletics and the performing arts. However, the idea that a coach can help improve performance outcomes for people in the workplace and other settings is relatively new. I believe that coaching is partnering with people in a thought-provoking and creative way that can inspire them to their greatest personal and professional potential. This honors my talent of Maximizer®, which seizes opportunities to help people become their very best.

When I decided to launch my own strength-based coaching practice in the fall of 2013, it quickly became apparent to me that I needed direction from someone to help me understand the approach needed to be successful. A Google search produced a list of coaches who had successful coaching practices utilizing the CliftonStrengths® assessment. I contacted a coach who had been successful for more than two decades and who wanted to coach new Gallup-Certified Strengths Coaches. Over the next two years, he provided me with critical insights into the coaching profession. He spent extensive time helping me understand how my unique talents would help me achieve success. Most importantly, he helped me understand how I could be an effective coach applying my distinctive strengths. I now find myself thinking how much success can someone achieve without a coach? I also wonder how successful can someone become in the twenty-first century without understanding their own unique excellence?

Job Crafting

One of my most gratifying coaching experiences was working with a client I will call Daniel. Daniel worked in a branch office of an IT firm headquartered in the northeast where he was the lone company representative in Columbus, Ohio. During our first meeting, he indicated he was lukewarm about his position. He also felt that the people working in the main office did not understand him and he was considering a job change due to insufficient opportunities to grow professionally.

Like most coaches, I feel it is important to expand my knowledge base in topics related to positive psychology and human development. Through research, I became interested in the concept of job crafting and the work undertaken by the Center for Positive Organizations at the University of Michigan and Dr. Amy Wrzesniewski.

According to the Center, job crafting is a means of describing the ways in which employees utilize opportunities to customize their jobs by actively changing their tasks and interactions with others at work. In Daniel's situation, he was interested in how strengths development could help him craft his job to avoid a needless job search. Initially, I encouraged Daniel to take the CliftonStrengths® assessment.

We spent our first sessions together working through the Daniel's talent profile. One of Daniel's dominant talents was Analytical®, where the individual desires large amounts of data to process and analyze. While he was effective at his job, he was looking for new challenges within the confines of his current position.

He was able to comprehend how his dominant strengths could help him interact with work colleagues from his remote location. He also discovered how to better utilize his talents to be more effective in his role in ways that brought more joy. He began to experience more meaningful interactions with his colleagues, too.

In spite of this, Daniel was still interested in leveraging his strengths to make his job even more to his liking while fulfilling his obligation to his employer. I was able to walk him through a series of exercises that helped him redesign his job. Part of the process was for him to analyze his primary assignments and redesign tasks and workflow in ways that allowed him to use more of his unique abilities at work. Through our time together, Daniel discovered several concrete steps he could take to improve his engagement and ultimately, envisioned a new future with his company.

We spend way too much time at work to be unhappy there. In my experience, mid-career changes are often difficult because people are settled into lifestyles and fear starting over, but they don't have to! Learning how your strengths are used in your current role and expanding them to do more of what you love can create career purpose and well-being.

Personal Mission Statement

While I enjoy the thrill of working with individuals, I get extra pleasure in working with teams, especially the smaller ones. Recently, I facilitated a four-hour workshop for a team of six college administrators at a large university in the Midwest. The team members work in the same academic department within the university. Out of the six-team members, half had worked in the department for an extended period while the remaining people were new to the department. The understanding of strengths development for each team member ran the gamut from very knowledgeable to novice. I came armed with books and resources to showcase the breadth of the strengths development movement.

During the first part of the workshop, I covered some of the basic concepts behind the CliftonStrengths® assessment and discussed ways to turn their talents into strengths. Using the Gallup Strengths Insight Guide, I had them select words and phrases from the reports that resonated with them under each of their talent themes. From there, I challenged the participants to create a personal mission statement that incorporated their dominant talents. What they discovered during this exercise is just how unique they are and what value they brought to the team.

Later, they shared their first drafts with one another. They began to understand the contributions of each member of the team. While they were sharing, they learned new things about one another and developed a strong desire to continue the process of growing together as a team.

While talent development is ultimately personal, the effects can drive team performance in powerful ways. A personal mission statement can help each person begin the process of understanding how their strengths dynamically work together and how those strengths can be leveraged to serve others.

Leveraging Strengths to Create Collaboration

A few years ago, I facilitated a workshop with a team of IT professionals who worked for an international car manufacturer. The new supervisor who invited me to join them was already familiar with the CliftonStrengths® assessment. He wanted to use it to learn about this new team and help them work together more effectively.

In my preparation, I discovered that half of the members were dominant in the talents of Deliberative® and Responsibility®. Both of these talents can be time-sensitive with a strong need to provide work that is both accurate and excellent. To some degree, the challenge for them was getting more lead-time on projects in order to accomplish better results. Knowing this, the supervisor was able to understand this need and was willing to adjust his timelines and deadlines. The team felt heard and it paved the way for better communication.

Another revelation was that the team lacked talents in the Influencing Domain of Leadership (Rath & Conchie, 2008). They were concerned that their contributions to the company were under-appreciated. Through the conversation, they brainstormed opportunities for other departments within their division to help them convey their success stories. They learned the importance of partnership, not only within their department but with supporting units on campus. They were able to identify other departments who they believed would be receptive to collaboration and sketched out a basic plan.

In my experience, it is common for groups or teams to discover the lack of specific strengths in their team's profile. After all, certain talents and strengths seem to be more suited for specific roles. These perceived deficiencies do not have to impede performance. Through coaching and training, learning how to lean into your unique excellence becomes a leveraging opportunity to serve others while accepting their contribution.

Twenty-First Century Career

My paternal grandfather worked for one construction firm for 40 years. My father worked for the Federal Reserve Bank for a few years before spending 25 years working for a rural Pennsylvania bank. My career includes over ten job changes to date. It's no secret that the Millennial generation will change jobs if they are not happy and satisfied in their current role. They also have an expectation to be coached, not managed.

The twenty-first century career will be a circuitous one with numerous job changes and career shifts, unlike the linear careers of previous generations. I truly believe strengths development provides answers for this complicated workforce environment.

In our current workforce circumstances, it is important to be able to manage your own career and understand your unique talents to move from one work environment to the next. The millennial generation and the generations that follow them will demand employers recognize their distinctive abilities and, more importantly, how to help them maximize their professional development.

I strongly believe that coaching individuals and teams utilizing positive psychology and strengths development can help transform the workplace to be more engaged and respectful of individual excellence. My hope for the twenty-first century is that people learn how to rely on their own unique excellence as they move forward in their career. It will allow them to acclimate to the new reality of frequent change and help them adapt quickly to new job circumstances.

About the Author

David G. Boop, Ed.D.

Context®, Responsibility®, Arranger®,
Individualization®, Maximizer®

David has been part of the strengths movement for more than 20 years. In addition to being a Gallup-Certified Strengths Coach, he has earned his Ed.D in Higher Education, is a Protean Career Coach and facilitator in the Dependable Strengths Articulation Process. With knowledge and experience in working at the collegiate level, David has worked extensively in career development roles, including teaching graduate level Positive Psychology courses. He is a public speaker, trainer and coach who works with individuals and teams.

You can reach David at:

Email: DavidBoop@hotmail.com
LinkedIn: www.linkedin.com/in/davidboop

Chapter Six - Kathie Gautille

....

PASSION AND PURPOSE
BRING LIFE

I grew up in the beautiful little town of Sewickley, outside of Pittsburgh, PA. I began working soon after graduating from Clarion University with a Bachelor's Degree in Communications with a concentration in Business. I worked for several different companies since graduating from college, and eventually was transferred to Dallas, Texas. While I truly enjoyed my career as a product manager for a software company, I chose to devote the next 14 years to my most challenging and rewarding career as a wife and mother of three children. When I returned to the workforce, I was ready to make a difference and soon found many opportunities for meaningful service.

Over the years, I discovered my passion for education and not just for my own children but for all children. I was led to run for an open seat on the local school board. I was elected four times, and had the honor and privilege to serve 12 years on the Coppell School Board. In addition to being a board member, I was elected by my peers to serve as President. I became a principal spokesperson for the board and together, we championed a more rigorous curriculum for students. During my tenure, we raised 90% of our campuses to the highest designation that a school can possess in the state of Texas. My service to the school district as a public servant, coupled with becoming a Master School Board Trustee with the Texas Association of School Boards fulfilled my desire to be a servant leader and my strong passion for children and education.

My desire to make a difference really peaked when I was Vice President of Marketing & Development for a Christian nonprofit. My team was responsible for developing and sustaining relationships within the community and helped move this Christian non-profit into one of the top nonprofits in the Dallas/Ft. Worth metro area. However, more importantly, I developed a strong desire to put my energy into causes. I felt it was my mission to bring higher awareness, meaning, and purpose to those most in need in my community. Passion and purpose are paramount to my well-being and me.

Embracing Who I Am

A new pastor was assigned to the church I had been attending for years. He was interested in growing an engaged parish and had used CliftonStrengths® at his last church. Our pastor wanted the leadership team to go through training based on the book, *Living Your Strengths* (Winseman, Clifton, & Liesveld, 2004), and I was fortunate enough to be part of that group. He believed that when an individual knows her strengths, she would also recognize how best to contribute to the church—identifying time, talent and treasure. Now, go one-step further and imagine an entire congregation being inspired to be more actively involved in the church, community and giving. The engagement would be tremendous. I was excited to be part of this endeavor.

After taking the assessment, I had the opportunity to have a coaching session with a Gallup-Certified Strengths Coach. Through the questions and conversation, I began to have greater clarity on my personality traits and really uncovered missing pieces that I never really understood. Coaching helped explain why I was such a passionate volunteer, why I always saw the silver lining in most circumstances, why math was such a chore for me, and why I loved mentoring.

One of the lessons that came to light after my first coaching session was my zest for life and people: my optimism, my love for all types of people, my love for just breaking the ice! For the first time ever, I was able to put a name to it and explain better what I already knew about myself as a working professional. I get energy when I am around people, when I talk with people, even total strangers, and I love to find out a little more about them. I have often acknowledged that I am a "people person" and that I began to realize the value I bring to a conversation or relationship as an active listener.

I knew some people enjoyed my high energy and enthusiasm, and some people were put off by it. I learned to modify the use of my talents to match and mirror the power of the client or friend in front of me. I call this "flexing my style." What I learned during my coaching session was understanding the dynamic energy, and the sheer power that takes place between my Woo®, Positivity®, and Individualization® talents. This self-awareness allows me to be more effective in my communication, as well as be in tune with the people around me.

Through the process of taking the assessment and participating in coaching, I've come to understand who Kathie Gautille is. Instead of being disappointed in the need to acknowledge the things I am not, I instead genuinely embrace who I am.

From Ministry to Business

After going through my initial training, I spent the next three years coaching predominantly at my church. I loved working with faith-based committees, councils, ministries, and individuals. I wanted more than anything for members of our church that I coached to have the blessing of an "ah-ha" experience, and know how they could contribute to our faith community. As I got more involved in the strengths movement, I found myself being called upon to take a deeper dive into coaching.

Often after I facilitated a church workshop, a participant would approach me about conducting a workshop for his/her business. As ludicrous as this may sound, this created turmoil inside of me. I saw my strengths coaching as a ministry, not a business. However, after working with another professional strengths coach, I was able to see that I could actually do both! One of the best decisions I've ever made was to move forward and become a Gallup-Certified Strengths Coach!

I was able to partner with someone whose talents were high in the Strategic Thinking Domain (Rath & Conchie, *Strengths Based Leadership: Great Leaders, Teams, and Why People Follow*, 2008) and put together my business plan. I hammered out my branding, my web design, my logo, and finally put my shingle out as a Gallup-Certified Strengths Coach, because I was now open for business!

Pivotal Coaching Moments

One of my favorite coaching experiences was working with a seasoned senior level manager who contacted me for real direction. She was having a crisis in confidence. After working for a major corporation, she was being forced to resign. She had spent over 25 years of her career with this company and she couldn't see beyond this decision that was thrust upon her unexpectedly.

After looking at her CliftonStrengths® results, we began to unpack her talent themes. We took a closer look at how they were helping or hurting her in her personal and professional life. What she discovered was that her talents were mostly in the Strategic Thinking and Influencing Domains, which made her very strong in critical thinking and Big Picture planning (Rath & Conchie, *Strengths Based Leadership: Great Leaders, Teams, and Why People Follow*, 2008). Her challenge was that she lacked some interpersonal skills to convey her ideas in a way that brought consensus.

Her pivotal moment came when she recognized that her critical thinking or strategic talent themes often overpowered her relationship themes, preventing her from gaining buy-in from the rest of her team. Through the exercises we worked on during our coaching sessions, she was able to discover that just because she saw solutions quickly, she still needed to become more aware that she may "dismiss" people and their ideas and contributions, which could inadvertently devalue them in the process. She was finally able to come to the awareness of how important it was for her to acknowledge ideas, concepts and processes other members of her team brought to a project. This was a tremendous learning moment.

By the end of our coaching sessions, she discovered an entirely new career awaited her. She felt confident again, and knew she would be successful at the new endeavor. We were able to identify her strengths and how she could use them in the next chapter of her life. She had a greater understanding of who she was and how she could continue to develop into the very best version of herself.

It's clients' experiences like this that bring me joy!

Getting Unstuck

On New Year's Eve a few years ago, a woman in her mid-forties contacted me after taking the CliftonStrengths® assessment and learning her dominant talent themes. Before she hired me, I asked her why she wanted a strengths coach. She told me she was "stuck" and needed help to understand why. She shared that she had just written down her New Year's Resolutions and discovered that they were the same as the previous two years. She had not made any progress moving forward over the past three years! No wonder she felt stuck!

She's the executive director of a very small Christian non-profit. What we discovered through our coaching sessions was that she loved networking and connecting people and was exceptionally good at it! Her talents of Woo® and Communication® made her warm and friendly and gave her the ability to promote her organization.

However, when it came down to actually getting things done, nothing happened. Her biggest challenge was being able to execute on the promises she made to herself and others. As we went through her talent profile, we also learned that the majority of the talents from the Executing Domain were outside of her dominant themes (Rath & Conchie, *Strengths Based Leadership: Great Leaders, Teams, and Why People Follow*, 2008). This explained a great deal about why she wasn't moving forward.

Our first critical conversation was about her lack of collaboration with others. She needed to partner with others in order to help fill in her executing gaps. She was trying to do it all on her own, but clearly that wasn't working. Helping her learn the strength in partnerships was going to make her successful. I was able to guide her in breaking down the tasks she needed to accomplish. Her amazing networking skills aided her in finding individuals who could assist her. While at times this was a painstaking process, she began to embrace the concept of partnerships and knew this was a new beginning for her.

Next up, we examined her goals. She wanted to be a more dynamic evangelist for her Christian non-profit. She was new in her faith walk and soon learned that her enthusiasm was not enough. She needed education in order to take her ministry to the next level.

An opportunity came about for her to meet Ravi Zacharias, a well-known International Evangelist whom she deeply admired. My biggest fear was that her Activator® talent would cause her to "fly by the seat of her pants," and not prepare for the brief meeting she was granted and waste a fantastic opportunity.

I asked her to give serious consideration to the question: "What two things do you want him to know about you?" I also invited her to research his books and events so that she could honestly connect with him about what she appreciated about his work. I wanted him to have a good impression of who she was as a student of faith. I will tell you that was a hard conversation. It was a very personal conversation. I am confident she was not very happy at the end of our discussion. A coach isn't always going to tell you what you want to hear. In fact, a coach must be willing and able to have difficult conversations when necessary, in order to move the client forward.

After the weekend, she had exciting news! Not only did she get to meet her esteemed mentor, he invited her to spend a week in England at Oxford to attend one of his workshops. An all-expense paid workshop! She believed that it was preparation for the meeting that allowed her to capitalize on the opportunity. This woman has gone on to be accepted at Oxford University and into the Oxford Centre for Christian Apologetics, where she completed her second year. Next year she will graduate with her degree in Theology from Oxford.

Enhancing Communication for Couples

A young newlywed couple at church contacted me about being coached on their top talent themes. Initially, the husband was looking for career direction and his new wife wanted to explore her own strengths and weaknesses. I began one-on-one coaching, helping both independently discover how they were wired.

I really enjoyed getting to know them individually. I suspected from their CliftonStrengths® results that they were possibly polar opposites. Karen had Influencing and Relationship Building talents, while Philip was dominant in the Strategic Thinking Domain (Rath & Conchie, *Strengths Based Leadership: Great Leaders, Teams, and Why People Follow*, 2008). That meant that Karen was social, and Philip was a deep thinker! I'm sure you can imagine the potential problems they could encounter through their marriage if they didn't understand this about one another.

After going through the discovery of their talents, I inquired as to whether there was anything specific they wanted to address. They both expressed concerns about being understood by their spouse.

Karen was concerned that her husband didn't enjoy socializing. She was trying to understand why Philip did not want to go out with friends as often as she would like to as a couple. She also confided that she was hurt that he would spend so much time in his study, alone. Clearly, there were things brewing under the surface.

I brought them together to go through each of their dominant talent themes. I kicked things off by asking her husband if he is always thinking and did he find it difficult to turn off all of the cognitive activity? I knew his talent themes of Intellection® and Ideation®

kept his brain busy. Philip was able to share with his wife why he felt the need to be alone. It didn't have anything to do with her! This revelation allowed Karen to see that he wasn't shunning her or locking her out, but rather he needed his alone time in order to process. For him, thinking is doing.

With Karen's talents of Individualization®, Empathy® and Maximizer®, I knew from our earlier coaching session that she led with her feelings. I was curious how often she spoke to her friends and family on the phone. She was able to share with Philip how important it was to stay connected. For Philip, staying engaged with people was not a high priority.

This paved the way to learn how they received energy. Philip's talent combination obviously made him an introvert, and he recharges his batteries by being alone. On the other hand, Karen's high need for people made her an extrovert and she got her energy from others.

Independence in marriage can at times be a double-edged sword in the sense that you have to communicate what you need from another person, but you also need to be flexible in your expectations. For these reasons, communication is essential.

I invited Philip to appeal to Karen's Empathy® talent to be kind and sensitive when expressing his need to be alone so that she would not feel rejected. In addition, while Karen was learning not to take Philip's alone time so personally, she asked him he if would consider putting a time limit on his thinking. Conversely, because Karen needed to establish "couple" relationships with Philip, I suggested that perhaps they could agree to compromise on the frequency in which they go out with friends.

Six months after coaching this sweet couple, they reached out to me to say that they both understand better who they are individually, and as a couple. Embracing the differences rather than fighting them had made life so much happier since they learned their strengths!

In my experience in working with many couples, I have found the CliftonStrengths® assessment to be very instrumental in helping couples understand who they are and what they each bring to the relationship. It enhances communication for couples because it provides a language through which to understand their differences. Many couples already know they have this diversity in strengths, but this tool provides them with the words they may need to express it.

Value and Vulnerability

While giving a CliftonStrengths® leadership workshop to a team of marketing executives, I wanted each of them to explore the various ranges of their talents. I asked them to select two of their top talent themes, preferably one they knew well, and one they didn't under-stand as well, or perhaps didn't see in themselves. I invited them to share what they discovered in their small group.

As a way to begin this exercise, I explained the value and vulnerability of each of the talent themes. We need to consider how we manage our strengths, and the possible ways others may be understanding them. This begins with grasping that each of our strengths can become a weakness.

The three groups began sharing. I was periodically called over to help explain a talent theme members didn't understand or see in themselves. Each question and follow up answer provided a great learning experience.

As an example, one of the gentlemen did not see his Harmony® talent present at all. Not only that, he confessed that he didn't like the fact that he even had Harmony® as one of his dominant talents! When I was called upon to clarify, I turned to his peers, and said, "Let me ask each of you, how do you see his Harmony® talent in action?" They were able to show him how this talent manifested as a strength in him, and for the team. I went on to do this with other team members and their talents. It became a powerful exercise in affirming the positive in each other.

The biggest take away was everyone understanding the full range in which their talent themes can manifest themselves. When operating in value, they bring their best to the team. When operating in vulnerability, their talent can become a hindrance, and thus not provide the greatest benefit to themselves and others. Self-awareness is essential to being a contributing member of a team.

Fearfully and Wonderfully Made

As a woman of faith, I believe what is said in Psalm 139:14, "I praise you because I am fearfully and wonderfully made: Wonderful are your works; my very self you know."

I believe God has created each of us in such a way that our passions, desires, and the things that truly bring us joy are unique. The first time I was coached on my strengths, I began to really understand that what I can give to the world is a blessing; a gift to be used for good. I found it very liberating that I no longer had to live like other people wanted me to, and I could let go of the things that I was not. I learned to embrace all of me. I need to use the talents God gave me. That began with truly understanding myself, which CliftonStrengths® helped me to see.

I believe helping people see they are "fearfully and wonderfully made" is one of the most important things I can do with my strengths as a coach! I love helping individuals find the confidence and self-love they lost or misplaced! I really believe being a coach is a calling for me.

About the Author

Kathie Gautille

Woo®, Arranger®, Belief®, Positivity®, Individualization®

Kathie Gautille is a global, faith-based coach who works with executives and teams, in the nonprofit, corporate and faith-based sectors. She is an expert at helping leaders discover their passion and purpose. She has held many leadership roles that have given her a depth of knowledge and experience to develop best practices in coaching organizational teams.

Kathie is a Gallup-Certified Strengths Coach and has clients both domestic and abroad, which makes her an "in demand" strengths coach.

You can reach Kathie at:

Email: Kathie@KathieGautille.com
Website: www.KathieGautille.com
LinkedIn: https://www.linkedin.com/in/kathiegautille/
IG handle: @leadwithstrength
FB: https://m.facebook.com/kathiegautillestrengthscoach-ing/

Chapter Seven - Beverly Griffeth-Bryant

DRIVEN TO DESIGN AND ENGAGE

A t the time I began my strengths journey I was a full-time Training Specialist, for the Northern District of Illinois Bankruptcy Court. My role is to design, develop and facilitate technical training programs for court unit employees, attorneys, trustees and their staff.

Since 2004, our leadership has endeavored to embark on a mission to improve employee engagement so that employees are enthusiastic and involved in their work. We began our journey of discovering and exploring our strengths. I completed the CliftonStrengths® assessment and the moment had arrived to discover my most dominant talents.

Wow! As I read the reports and the descriptions of my potential strengths, many events from my past came rushing to my mind. Includer® explained how often I would get strange looks when planning an event when I asked who should also be included, either in the planning or in participation of an event. It also explained my dislike for cliques.

Initially, I had difficulty understanding my Strategic® talent. I took a deep dive into its description and spent time observing my daily life to discover where I could see this talent in play. I realized that much of my time is spent thinking about whatever the task I want to complete.

I was thinking about how to make the most significant impact in a training program, thinking about who would be participating, and how I could give them helpful and useful tips to create success in a new role. I realized that I think a lot about the content and activities of my workshops or employee training programs.

My Belief® talent took me back to Detroit, Michigan, where as a teenager I was very active in political and charitable organizations. My inner core values are the foundation of everything I do, including my decision to become a Gallup-Certified Strengths Coach. It also has driven me to take on the mission of my court unit to keep the strengths conversation alive.

The very core of the strengths movement is about helping people discover their very best, and to leverage their best at work and in their lives. The assessment results provide an individual with a new lens or a prescription through which to view life, relationships and an understanding of how they operate in those areas. As a coach, I have the privilege to come alongside an individual and help them see a perspective of themselves that they were most often unaware of and to help them leverage the new-found knowledge going forward.

My Positivity® talent is my personality anchor that helps me find something to laugh or smile about no matter the situation. I recall once being told that I am "like a mighty rushing wind." Someone from my church actually said to me, "When you enter a room, you bring a great energy into the room. And when you leave the room, it goes with you." I laughed at this because often times I do not see this in myself.

In my own strengths development, I have discovered that I am impatient with the status quo. I need to make something better than it was before. Understanding that this comes from my strong Maximizer® talent has been empowering.

Follow-up Honesty

One of my first self-discoveries occurred during a Hilltop Speakers Toastmasters® meeting. We were discussing how to reach out to past guests and visitors to our club. It was decided that we would divide the list of names among us and we would each make follow-up calls to encourage them to return. At the sound of learning that I would have to call complete strangers, I became very uncomfortable. In that moment, I had a significant "aha!" While this task sounded like a simple follow-up phone call to the other officers, to me it sounded like a sales pitch. I realized that the job was not in alignment with my talent theme of Relator®. I am comfortable sharing and influencing someone when I believe the information can be life-changing for him or her. Sharing my faith, helping someone know their strengths and helping them leverage them in their job-these are some routine situations that are naturally comfortable for me. Because I understood who I am and how I operate best, I was able to pass on the task at hand and apply my talents for our club in different areas.

Working Through Resistance

Early in my strengths journey, I participated in the Federal Court Leadership Program. This is when I realized that my CliftonStrengths® talent of Belief® was not operating at maximum performance. My leadership project was to create a practical path for my court unit, and other court units in the judiciary, to implement the strengths-based approach to our organization. I needed a group of employees to help in brainstorming, creating and testing the plan.

My initial strategy was to form a focus group to work with the training team. My reasoning was that this team could develop an awareness of their strengths, transform their talents into strengths, and leverage those newly acquired strengths in the role of mentors and coaches to others in the court unit. I had a meeting with my team and our manager and shared what I thought would be their role as the focus group. The team was asked to provide their thoughts or let me know if they had any questions. At the time, there were no objections.

I scheduled and held the second meeting, reviewing strengths activities, clarifying strengths terms and gave the first focus group assignment. I felt encouraged about the second meeting and the start of the focus group project. Unfortunately, that was short lived. As the days went by, I began to receive resistance from the members of the focus group as I attempted to schedule our next meeting.

I began to discover that not everyone bought into the concept of focusing on transforming talents into strengths and managing around weaknesses. Some members felt that the strengths-based initiative was just another initiative to come and go. Some thought that strengths-based management was an excellent idea, but personally, they did not want to develop the roadmap for the organization. Wow! Where did I go wrong?

My first realization was that my Maximizer® talent is driven and passionate about the strengths-based concept. I assumed that everyone felt like I did! Secondly, realized that I never asked how they felt about participating in the strengths focus group!

Feeling deflated, I regrouped and began researching how to sell an idea to an organization. I sent an email out to the court unit, asking if anyone was interested in joining a strengths focus group. What a novel idea! This email generated 12 volunteers for the strengths focus group. Now I had the right people, people who were excited about strengths-based development!

Keeping the Conversation Alive

This initial focus group became the strengths champions of our organization. We had to find a way to keep the strengths conversation alive. Through brainstorming around their ideas, we developed Talent Tuesday, a monthly meeting where people join us and learn more. It was a resounding success!

Three years after we began that program, I started thinking about how we could take it to the next level. I recognized that we were missing many people because working remotely was becoming popular. Some employees were no longer coming into the office regularly and were missing our learning sessions. Moreover, I wanted to share our journey beyond our court unit.

This is when an online version of Talent Tuesday was born! Our monthly program, which started with a handful of people sitting in a circle in a training room, has now reached more than 1,000 people. Many have identified how they are leveraging their talents and strengths in their roles, and others have determined which new jobs are, or are not, a fit for them. They have also discovered new things about their peers and co-workers that they never knew. Keeping the conversation centered on strengths has proven powerful and effective.

Answering the Call to Coach

As we began implementing processes in the court unit, I was able to have a coaching session with a strengths coach. My coaching session was unlike any experience I had ever had! The session focused on me, with questions that challenged me to think about how I saw my talents and where I had experienced them in action. This coaching session lit inside of me a desire to become a coach.

I knew at this point that becoming a strengths coach would be an important step in my development. Unfortunately, this was beyond the scope of my budget. Undaunted, I continued to look for a way and found one within the faith-based division of Gallup®, which existed at that time. While my employer was unable to fund my training, I chose to move forward anyway. My Belief® talent pushed me into action. I knew I was called to be a strengths coach! I was determined to make it happen and I did, even at my own personal cost.

Job Crossroads

One my most significant coaching experiences was actually with my niece. At the time, she was at a crossroads in her life and career. She was frustrated in her current job and wanted to find a role that she could love or at least enjoy going to each day.

We started with looking at her dominant talents and her Gallup Strengths Insight Report. I invited her to read and highlight the words, phrases or sentences that resonated with her. Then, I asked her questions about her highlights and when had she experienced the thought, feeling or behavior of each talent, or saw these themes in action. To her surprise, she could see herself in most of them. Her CliftonStrengths® talent of Ideation® explained why she is a voracious writer.

She has written plays and fiction books with interesting characters and storylines since she was a little girl. While she has never had them published, she loves to spend hours writing about her ideas. Often, she's not able to sleep until all her thoughts and ideas have been put to paper.

She is also dominant in the talent of Woo®, which stands for "winning others over." This explains her ability to convince a person of anything, especially meaningful things that have purpose. Paired with her Communication® talent, she uses words to influence others. She loves working in a team environment or a job where meeting and communicating with people is a big part of her role.

One of the strengths she did not instantly identify in herself was the CliftonStrengths® talent of Strategic®. She told me, I am not a planner. I began our discussion by having her look at the theme description. She highlighted, "take the time to fully reflect or muse about a goal to achieve until the related patterns and issues emerge for you" and "when the time comes, seize the moment and state your strategy with confidence." I was able to help her see that this is a "thinking" talent and not necessarily a planning talent. In my experience, some people confuse their understanding of the name of the talent based on a presumed definition. Through coaching, we are able to allow them to discover these potential strengths within them.

After a full debriefing, we talked about how her newly acquired insights could be leveraged as she looked for a fulfilling position. I made it clear that the talents themselves don't suggest a particular job but offer insight on what might appeal to her job satisfaction and well-being. This would allow her to inquire about the working environment, and to learn what team life might look like at any new company she was considering. About a month later, I received a phone call from her, thrilled about the new job she had accepted! She would be working with a variety of customers, developing customer relationships and creating custom solutions for them daily. This new role appeared to be a perfect fit!

Overuse Can Lead to Overwhelm

I had the opportunity to coach a co-worker and friend who was struggling with the ability to say "No." She was experiencing a lot of stress, fatigue, and frustration because she found it increasingly difficult to turn down requests. People often asked her to complete tasks because they knew they could count on her. She often found herself overcommitted and over-extended. She was looking to learn how to avoid becoming constantly overwhelmed.

We began our discussion around her CliftonStrengths® talent of Responsibility®. She began to recognize her need to take ownership of all of her commitments. She also realized that she had an obsession to do things "right," which earned her the reputation for being dependable, but at what cost?

I began to ask her about how these requests came to her. Did she feel more pressure when asked in person, versus by phone or text? What about her time management? Did she make notes of new commitments? What she discovered was that she was saying "Yes!" to everything, regardless of whether it was in her best interest or not. This obviously set her up for potential failure, something that would have devastated her had it happened. Overusing a talent can have disastrous consequences.

Through our coaching sessions, we were able to create for her a new strategy: she would no longer accept any new responsibilities "on the spot." This would give her the opportunity to check her calendar and truly determine if the request was something she wanted to fulfill and could do so without pressure.

In my follow up, she informed me that the new strategy was working very well! On occasion, she still caught herself saying, "Yes," without thinking, but she would quickly correct herself. This new method of committing to new things kept the pressure off and made her workflow manageable.

Best in Class

I had the pleasure of coaching Josh, a technology professional who works in our divisional office. As we sat in his office talking about his talents, I learned that Josh was a Navy veteran who was awarded the Honorman in recognition for earning the highest GPA in his class. It was obviously a trend, because in college he also won multiple top awards for academics among student athletes.

I also discovered that Josh loves technology and endeavors to become the best at providing network security for our court unit and judiciary. He is excited by the latest security trends and feels the need to continue his education, which explained why he was in the process of completing his Master's Degree in Management Information Systems. His goal was to finish with a 4.0 GPA.

During our coaching sessions, Josh's dominate talents of Competition® and Achiever® stood out the most. Most competitors look to win against other people. I asked him how Competition® shows up for him. He said, "I compete with myself, not with other people-to see how much I can learn and achieve. I set goals for myself, some of which I miss, but it keeps me moving forward towards achievement." For Josh, his interest was in competing with himself to be the "best in class." Achievement was critical for him to consider himself winning.

Because of the uniqueness of each person and the dynamic interplay of his or her individual talents, the talent profile is ultimately personal. Through coaching and training, each person has the opportunity to discover and embrace their own strengths identity. Being sensitive to the way someone perceives his or her own talents is essential.

Vision for the Future

Ever since I can remember, well-meaning friends and family, schools, and workplace managers have told us what we need to do in order to be successful. No matter what the advice, it always came back to fitting someone else's mold. If you're like me, you've spent most of your life looking, searching for that role where you could leverage your unique best. At the foundation of everyone's journey to become successful, I believe we should begin with a discovery of who you are naturally.

I have taken many assessments that have attempted to explain who I am as a person. The CliftonStrengths® assessment, however, provided for me a clear, deep understanding of how I am uniquely wired to think, feel, behave and function in the world. I would encourage everyone to make the investment in yourself in personal development. Find a strengths coach to come alongside you who will shine a light in a place that may have been hidden from you.

Can you imagine what your life and the lives of those around you could be if you knew, understood, appreciated and applied how you are uniquely talented?

About the Author

Beverly Griffeth-Bryant
Includer®, Strategic®, Belief®, Positivity®, Maximizer®

Since 2015, Beverly Griffeth-Bryant has been a Gallup-Certified Strengths Coach and has worked in the federal courts for the last 32 years. She serves in the United States Bankruptcy Court as a Training Specialist.

She and other strengths champions in the court unit strive to weave strengths-based language through new employee orientation, coaching, and innovative training. She's been married to Michael for 27 years and has one son, Eric Michael.

You can reach Beverly at:

LinkedIn: Beverly Griffeth-Bryant
Twitter: EverydayTalents2Strengths, Talents2Strengths
Email: talents2strengths@gmail.com

Chapter Eight - Murray Guest

BE INSPIRED THROUGH STRENGTHS

L eaving school, I studied biology. I liked it at school, and I think like many people, because I loved a subject at school, I might as well find out more about it! This study led me to the wine industry for a season and then into food technology, where I started working for an International food company, Mars Inc.

I ended up working for Mars for the next eleven years and look fondly at my time there. They are a global family-owned business whose culture is grounded in the five principles of quality, responsibility, efficiency, mutuality, and freedom. My talents for attention to detail, serving others, communication and continuous improvement combined with their outstanding professional development program led me from the factory into Quality Assurance.

At school, I never thought I'd be a Quality Assurance Manager, a role which I loved. But, if I didn't follow my heart and do what I love doing, I may never have ended up there. At this point in my career, I wasn't aware of CliftonStrengths®. However, I can now see I was focusing on my natural talents and turning them into strengths. As a parent, one of the most rewarding things is helping your children identify their natural talents and follow their passions. Take time to reflect on how you can do this and guide them towards fulfillment in their lives.

Passion for Developing Others

After leaving Mars, Inc., I realized one of my passions was helping others develop and be their best self. I approached Amazing People, a training company that I admired. I was hired as a facilitator where I deepened my understanding of communication, coaching, teamwork, and leadership. At Amazing People, I experienced strengths-based leadership.

As a company, they embraced the uniqueness of individuals, providing them opportunities to shine and apply their talents and strengths. For example, team members and trainers were matched to roles where they could be their best selves and form collaborative partnerships on training programs. Roles in business development and program logistics were also matched to people's talents. This created a high-performance culture where team members were engaged, creative and we had a lot of fun!

After three years, an opportunity became available to manage Learning and Development for an aluminum smelter with nearly 1,200 employees.

This role gave me the opportunity to apply my knowledge and experience in systems and people development. Looking back at leading the team of trainers over this time, I can see how I aimed my Individualization® talent to develop my team and match the needs of the organization with their skills. As a result, we were honored at the Hunter Manufacturing Awards, being recognized for Excellence in Training.

During the next stage in my career, I joined a training organization that provides psychology-based safety training. In essence, we were helping high-risk companies build cultures where everyone goes home safely every day by focusing on leadership and attitudes. I facilitated dozens of workshops and partnered with many leaders, and this is where I was introduced to the CliftonStrengths® assessment.

As part of my employee induction, I received a copy of the Tom Rath book *StrengthsFinder 2.0*. I connected immediately with the strengths-based approach and all the benefits it brings. I dived into the book and soaked up all the information, embracing my dominant talent themes. I could see how they had been part of who I was as a leader, father, husband and young boy growing up at school, which led me to claim them as my own.

At the beginning of 2015, I started my own business and became a Gallup-Certified Strengths Coach! I have now worked with over 1,200 people, helping them claim and aim their strengths!

CliftonStrengths® provides the ideal language, framework and process to unlock people's talents, increase self-awareness and a deeper understanding of others. This understanding transforms relationships, teams, culture and performance. It helps people let go of the past and move forward to a place of greater collaboration, creativity, and innovation to create a culture where team members embrace the differences in each other. Every conversation is an opportunity to lift others up and help them be the best version of themselves. Simply put, every interaction is an opportunity to influence organizational culture in a positive way.

When Talent Becomes a Weakness

I think one of my most significant insights has been understanding that my weaknesses are my strengths in a raw, or misdirected application. Also, that I'm okay! The realization that I don't need fixing, and that some of the perceptions of myself that I'd taken on from others, were only their perceptions. It was empowering to me. Through understanding my talent themes and the strengths of them, I gained more self-confidence and belief in myself. All through school, I was the kid who couldn't stop talking in class. Report after report highlighted the weakness of this trait and its disruption to the other students, led me to rush my work and had me in trouble for not focusing. It also showed up early in my career where I was waiting to speak in conversations and was not actively listening. To see the talent of Communication® revealed as one of my dominant strengths, I was not surprised, but I was actually a little relieved. This misdirected talent had been a thorn in my side for so long, it was inspiring to know that I could claim, develop and own this misdirected talent.

As a leader, when a team member would share their story of woe and troubles, I could feel myself tuning out of the conversation and not showing them the attention they deserved. My thoughts would jump to questions like "What are you doing about this? How can you move on? What's in your control? How can we prevent this from happening again?"

What I've discovered is that showing empathy is not my natural reaction and to demonstrate it and make people feel heard I need to apply more intentional focus and energy. I was not surprised to discover that the CliftonStrengths® talent of Empathy® is one of my lesser strengths. Don't forget, we can apply all of the 34 CliftonStrengths® talents, it just takes more focus and energy to apply our lesser ones.

I still remember vividly a conversation and the big "aha" moment in a coaching session with a senior leader as he was understanding the concept of strengths as weakness. He had claimed Relator® and had this realization of how if he didn't connect with someone, well, as he put it "I just wipe them off my radar." I asked him, "How's this working out for you?" He replied, "Well, it's not. I've got broken or ineffective relationships with my peers and team members." In exploring the dark and light of his strengths and developing an action plan to improve the regulation of them, combined with conscious leadership, he was able to improve the relationships and started to appreciate others more.

Flow State through Strengths

There is nothing quite like being in a "state of flow." It's that feeling of being in "the zone," energized, instinctively knowing what to do next and connected to what you're doing. For me, it's when I'm coaching leaders or facilitating workshops. In these activities, I get to "feed" my strengths.

I've realized my calling to coach is just who I am. It shows up in the way I talk to clients, family, and friends. It's a calling to serve others, to help them see what's possible and how they can get there. My dominant strengths have the opportunity to shine!

I'm able to identify the uniqueness in individuals, build relationships, help them see what's possible in their future and serve them to be their best.

To help you embrace your strengths, reflect on the times when you were in a "state of flow" and what strengths were being used and nurtured. What were you doing and how were you feeling? From there, look to create future opportunities where you can do more of this.

An example of this is in how I use one of my strongest talents, Relator®. Something I've always been able to do quite naturally is connect with others and build relationships. Understanding this in the framework of the work of Donald O. Clifton, the creator of the CliftonStrengths® assessment, I've reflected and identified how I've been able to use it in a powerful way and turn it into a strength. At my core is a desire for deep, authentic relationships; relationships built on trust, openness, and honesty.

For me, my Relator® talent is all about building relationships with clients that are based on mutual trust and connection. The majority of relationships with my clients go far beyond transactional. Friendships are formed with open discussions of family and more significant life topics. I know this strength has contributed to my business success.

When are you in a state of flow? Notice how it feels and what talents you are getting to apply. Take some time to reflect on how to create more opportunities to be in this state and create this feeling.

A Change in Approach

A rewarding coaching experience I had was with a leader in the manufacturing industry. He was new to his role as the CEO of a large organization. His industry reputation and experience saw him perfectly suited for the role. It was a position where changes were needed in the corporate culture and client base to achieve the growth expectations of the board of directors. He also had grand visions for the organization, visions of increased production, market share, increased work with current clients and some specific new clients.

In our conversations, the significant challenges he was facing became apparent. One of the greatest obstacles he had was in getting the employees to see his vision and be engaged in the process. He was frustrated in their perceived resistance, not getting "onboard" and this was also creating tension in the management team. He struggled in relating to the historical journey of the employees, which inhibited building relationships. Without intervention, employee turnover was destined to increase, engagement to decrease and the grand visions never being realized.

Through coaching sessions, he became aware of his dominant Futuristic® and Achiever® talents, they combined for him to see what is possible, how to get there and gave him the confidence that drove him to take action. He knew what could be achieved! His strong Self-Assurance® talent theme was helping this, but it also led to perceptions of him appearing arrogant and overconfident.

What he discovered about himself was that he wasn't bringing people on the journey. He also wasn't creating followers to his vision, and this was causing frustration in the team. Through coaching and building his self-awareness, he realized the need to invest more time earlier in communicating the vision and the "why." He provided that through greater context and asking for input, and this enabled the entire team to find the way forward. This change in approach not only helped achieve the plan, it improved employee engagement and reduced his stress, too.

Strength in Vulnerability

It takes a lot of courage and vulnerability to apologize to your team. However, one leader I coached did just that. Prior to the coaching experience, with little self-awareness of the impact of his behaviors, he had no idea of the damage he was inflicting on his team. Through our coaching relationship, he had the realization that he was over-playing a combination of his dominant talents.

The realization of the impact this was having on his team's morale and engagement was a significant breakthrough. Because of his CliftonStrengths® Analytical® and Deliberative® talents, he had the need to analyze and deliberate excessively. This caused frustrations, a slowness to act, extreme risk adversity and even a mistrust of others. He was able to recognize that his own "analysis paralysis" was damaging the corporate culture. It was inspiring how he "owned it" and embraced that he needed to take action to turn things around. Trust is the foundation of all effective teams, and as the work in *Dysfunctional Teams* by Patrick Lencioni has shown, one of the best ways to rebuild trust is to be vulnerable (2010).

Through coaching sessions and the process of claiming his strengths, this amazing leader invested time and energy in regulating his dominant talents more productively. This was combined with heartfelt sessions of vulnerability, which included apologizing to his teams. This leadership, combined with team strengths workshops, shifted the culture dramatically. There was improved trust, openness, and team members began leveraging the talents of each other.

When can you be more vulnerable to build trust?

Stronger Relationships through Strengths

"Can I get my partner to do the CliftonStrengths® assessment?" is the one question I've been asked many times. Even in corporate team workshops! It's in that moment when a participant realizes the information in front of them is providing insights not only about themselves, but also their partner at home.

One participant recalled a story of what it looks like when they go on vacation and the stress that happens every time they plan for their family holiday. Her husband has a very specific approach to pack the caravan, the equipment, and the supplies in a very methodical and exact way. His CliftonStrengths® talent of Discipline® were always very much in play. Then, he would plan every step of the journey, including all the activities they would explore.

His wife, who had none of these organizing, consistent, focused talents as part of her strengths profile, always felt like her need for adventure and spontaneity was being squashed. She now realized how she wasn't acknowledging the positives of her husband's approach. They began to have amazing conversations about the more flexible and unstructured tendencies brought with her talents of Adaptability® and Ideation®.

Helping couples understand the unique and diverse talents they each bring to their relationship can provide answers to common conflict. A deep understanding of one another's gifts can help them lean on each other more effectively. Instead of being "wrong," they now know they are merely different.

Improving Your Meetings through Strengths

Organizational teams generally don't meet frequently or regularly enough. Meetings with poor dynamics, no clear process, purpose or value are far too common. This, in turn, costs organizations billions of dollars globally in lost productivity. It also causes many team-members stress and frustration. Whether your team is stable, virtual, cross-functional or a project team, CliftonStrengths® provides a powerful tool to breathe new life and effectiveness into your meetings. Through knowing and embracing the talents of others, opportunities for people's strengths to shine are created. Meetings no longer need to be dysfunctional. Strengths can be matched to many different elements of the meeting. Some examples could be as follows: organizing the meeting, leading problem-solving discussions, and developing action plans. The process of getting to know each other more deeply through Clifton-Strengths® will also help the meetings improve.

I was working with a team of passionate teachers at Pre-K school. Each month, they would meet and discuss the upcoming projects for the children. Discussions would include the lesson plans, activities, locations, logistics, etc. One teacher would regularly ask questions in the meetings like "What if this happens? How will we keep the children safe? How will we manage the different activities at once?" Many team members, including the Director of the school, were getting frustrated with the questions. A common response to her questions was along the lines of, "Well, it will work out. Just get on board."

The teacher didn't feel heard, appreciated or respected. This led to her stress, poor performance, and disengagement. She was feeling like an outsider and really wanted to contribute. But she had given up.

Through strengths-based workshops, the team of teachers got to understand their own talents and learned how to appreciate the talents of other teachers. This new understanding led to leveraging each other's strengths and inquiring into their team member's perspectives from a strengths approach. Conversations at the monthly team meeting were much more productive with questions like "What possible problems do you think we need to manage for this project?" and thus valuing the team member's Restorative™ theme.

In addition, regular team meetings are an ideal vehicle to build your organizational strengths-based culture. Using the time when the team is together to integrate the language of CliftonStrengths® can be very effective in the meeting conversations. This will help embed strengths in your culture and encourage team members to recognize strengths in others. How could you integrate the language of strengths into your next team meeting?

The Personal Impact of Coaching
Toolbox meetings are conducted at the start of every shift in many high-risk operations in manufacturing, mining and construction industries. The meetings are a critical process to ensure operators are switched on and ready to complete the work of the shift ahead safely. Additionally, they support developing a continuous improvement culture.

Leaders often find these meetings difficult to facilitate, as is often said that public speaking is feared more than death! However, through understanding their talents and approaching the meetings through their strengths, leaders are able to build their confidence and skills to deliver effective and engaging meetings. I received an email from a participant about nine months after one of the Toolbox programs I had delivered. It was one of those emails that reassured me of the power and impact of being a strengths-based coach.

In the message, the participant described how his mother had recently passed away and as the oldest sibling, he needed to speak at her funeral. It is one of the most emotional times for a family, and I understood how he felt as my dad passed away only a year earlier. He went on to describe how, through applying what he had learned in the program the previous year, he was able to prepare and confidently deliver the eulogy at his mother's funeral. He referred to how he focused on the level of information he wanted to share, managing his emotions, the preparation process and applying his strengths as what helped him. His story and gratitude confirmed my calling as a coach and still fills my bucket as I reflect on the impact of his story.

Live an Inspired Life
My company's name is *Inspire My Business*, as I believe that everyone should have the opportunity to be inspired in all areas of their life. The conversations at home, in organizations, and with friends should be inspiring, uplifting, strengths focused, positive and energizing. Say "No!" to gossiping, dull discussions, to de-energizing tasks and responsibilities. I firmly believe, and

have witnessed, how a focus on strengths and all of the benefits a strengths-based approach brings will help create inspiring connections, conversations, relationships and teams.

Who can you inspire by recognizing their strengths today?

How will you be your best through achieving your goals through your strengths?

About the Author

Murray Guest
Relator®, Futuristic®, Individualization®,
Communication®, Responsibility®

Murray Guest is a Gallup-Certified Strengths Coach with more than 15 years' experience leading cultural change in large organizations. Combining his knowledge in shifting attitudes, leadership and a passion for strengths, Murray partners with business leaders to inject new energy into their organizations, and build an inspired culture that drives business performance and encourages success both personally and professionally.

He has helped over 1,200 people unlock their strengths and has worked with organizations to integrate strengths into their culture. Murray is in a state of flow when he is helping people embrace their full potential through either 1:1 leadership coaching or facilitating workshops. He loves mountain bike riding and having conversations that matter.

You can reach Murray at:

Website: www.inspiremybusiness.com
Email: inspire@inspiremybusiness.com

Chapter Nine - Donna Marie Gardner, M.A.

LEAP OF FAITH

We've all had a moment – a moment when you know that your life as you know it is going to change forever. In that moment you may feel exhilarated, frightened, off-balance, or maybe all three, but whatever the emotion, you know change is coming. I have had several of these moments in my lifetime, and my encounter with CliftonStrengths® was one of them.

My strengths journey is a deeply personal story. It is a story of self-awareness, healing, and above all, the story of a 65-year-old woman taking a leap of faith.

This is the story of a woman who faced a lot of change in her life, whose path was never straight. The story of a woman who sought security, continuity, and the familiar, but whose adult life delivered a very different experience. I was taught that "everyone has a story" and this is a glimpse into MY story. I share my story with you to set the stage for the profound impact CliftonStrengths® has had on my life and to illustrate that the positive effects of identifying one's talents can occur at any stage of life.

I have been blessed to have a long and varied career with lots of significant detours. It took a long time for me to see some of the detours as blessings – they often came veiled in what felt like a frightening challenge. I experienced the unexpected end of a long marriage, which led to the launch a new career. Later, the loss of a job required a move away from all that was familiar. Once again, the start of another career, after returning home to care for an aging father. None of these experiences were invited or sought out – yet they all offered new opportunity and new growth. Lots of growth!

I started my professional life as a high school teacher of language arts in an economically depressed community. I thought I would be teaching Shakespeare and George Bernard Shaw. Instead, I found myself teaching life skills and trying to help my students understand that they had value. I was 22 years old and a few of my students were 20! Some days it was terrifying.

After two years, I moved back to my hometown with my husband and pursued a graduate degree in Communication. I learned that communication skills were key factors in the way people influenced others, progressed toward goals and built relationships. It was an exciting time for me. I felt "lit up" and was driven to excel. Upon completion of my Master's degree, I had the opportunity to pursue a Ph.D. I declined. I wanted to have children and could not see how I could do both and do both well. I have never regretted that decision. For many years, I was blessed to have the opportunity to stay home and raise my children. I know what a gift that was for me! I filled my days with the activities of four active children – sports, dance and music lessons, and endless laundry. I sang in the church choir and was deeply engaged in community activities. I joined the Junior League, an international women's service organization, that provided me the opportunity to develop my leadership skills while making a positive difference in my community. Through the League, I was given the opportunity to teach, train and mentor others. I served on community boards and led non-profit board retreats. As a result of my community service, I was invited to co-author and facilitate the inaugural Community Leadership Development Academy in my hometown. I facilitated this program for several years.

This experience led me to begin working as a trainer for the local Community College, and ultimately the launch of my first business, a training company specializing in Communication and Leadership.

I worked part-time, enjoying the luxury of a flexible schedule that allowed me to continue to be active and present in the busy lives of my family.

Then, one day everything changed. I never expected to be one of the "statistics." I suspect no one does. Now, I was one. Divorced, single parent, female head of household - none of them sounded like me. However, they were me. Now, I needed full-time work with benefits! And so I began my next career as a non-profit fundraiser.

A New Career is Born

When I was offered my first position, I was shocked. I felt unprepared and out of my league. At that moment, I asked my new boss, "Did you read my resume? You do know that the most fundraising experience I have had is selling cookbooks and gala tickets, right?" His response seemed incredible to me. He said "I can teach you to fundraise. You have what I cannot teach. I see the qualities I need in you. You will succeed in this career." He hired me as the Director of Development for a statewide organization. My first year's goal was 2 million dollars! Yikes! What did he see in me that I did not see in myself?

My non-profit career spanned over two decades and he was right! I was a success. Across the span of my career, I raised funds for several non-profits and a university. I started this career thinking I was only capable of selling cookbooks and gala tickets, and ultimately had the opportunity to serve as the Vice President of a university! I was also able to continue to serve my community as a volunteer, chairing several community boards. All of this happened because someone saw TALENT in me that I did not see in myself.

When I retired from full-time work to care for my father, I was 62-years-old. I thought maybe I was finished working. Six months later, I knew I was not. I began to explore starting another business - this time focused on fundraising consulting, strategic planning, and Board Development training. When my father passed away at the age of 96, my consulting business was born.

Clues to Strengths

About the same time I started my consulting career, a colleague of mine (also a retired non-profit executive) started her consulting career. We had very different ways of approaching our new careers. She joined a prestigious consulting firm. I set up my laptop at my kitchen table and had my son design my business cards. She had a built-in clientele. I built mine through the relationships I had developed over the years. She had an office support system. I was a one-woman show.

After six months my friend quit her corporate consulting job. I was shocked! I loved doing what I was doing. Why didn't she? She told me that she hated having short-term contact with her clients. It frustrated her that she would give advice and sometimes they didn't take it. She hated that she couldn't see the projects all the way through! "How do you stand that, Donna?" she asked. And my response said it all - "That's exactly what works for me!"

I appreciate the excitement and challenge of new clients. I love getting things started and then I am okay handing it back to them. My comfort level working in this type of environment was a clue that I would soon identify as one of my core talents.

I was introduced to CliftonStrengths® when I was 65- years- old. Some may say – too old to benefit. After all, haven't we all been taught "you can't teach an old dog new tricks"?

I was hired to facilitate a board retreat for a non-profit organization, and the board chair handed me the StrengthsFinder 2.0 book by Tom Rath. She asked me to incorporate it into the retreat. That same week, in a strategic planning session with another client, I was handed the same book! Twice in one week people who knew me and valued me, both personally and professionally, placed this small book in my hands. Curious, I opened the book, went directly to the back, grabbed the code and took the assessment. The book could wait. I had to know why my colleagues thought this was so special. I quickly discovered my Activator® talent in action! Guided to seize opportunity in the moment, I jumped at the chance to learn what they were so excited about!

When I first viewed my results, I felt a rush of emotion. And there were tears, lots of tears. I was filled with emotion I could not contain. I sat and stared at that list of five words… my gifts… and tried to absorb them. Before reading the descriptions, I simply tried to let it soak in that these words had meaning, and that I gave them their meaning by living them. These words represented my greatest potential and my responsibility. I was blessed. It was there in black and white on a page in front of me. I had value.

Lest you think I am overdramatic, I am merely describing the pure "feelings" that poured over me. Intellectually, I knew I had value: I had raised four amazing children, managed a home, built a successful career, was a community leader and had lots of friends. But there was something about seeing those words on the page that tapped into a part of my life that was full of pain and uncertainty, and those five words on the page were balm to the hurt.

If I had only known 25 years ago that I had these gifts, I would have been much better armed to present myself in the workplace after my years at home with children. I would have had the confidence of knowing my gifts and the words to use to describe them, to "sell" them to prospective employers. I would have had confidence I so desperately needed at that fragile time in my life. At that moment, I knew I had to learn more. I wanted to share this gift with others.

As I studied my talent profile, a few things became surprisingly apparent. For years, one of the principle functions of my work was to facilitate strategic planning sessions. I never really understood how I fell into this type of work, or why, when facilitating a meeting with brilliant people, I seemed to be able to see the plan well ahead of everyone else. I knew I wasn't smarter, and now I had answers. My Strategic® talent theme allowed me to identify relevant patterns and issues quickly. My brain really did work differently than others.

Over time, I have come to understand that these talents have always been with me. Sometimes they have gotten in my way. Sometimes they have served me. I now know that the CEO who first hired me to be a fundraiser, despite my lack of experience, somehow saw these gifts in me. He sensed that I was a people person, a trust builder, an idea generator. He somehow knew that I could influence, engage and build strategy.

I have learned through personal experience that having a talent does not guarantee success. These talents are raw potential – innate, yes, but they require a lot of honing! I could look back on my life and see where my talents had often led me down a challenging path. My Ideation® talent theme often generates too many ideas without enough action!

The Leap

Once I was introduced to CliftonStrengths®, I could not ignore its gravitational pull. I immersed myself in reading about it. I bought book after book and began building a network of people who were involved in the strengths movement. A few of my clients bravely let me introduce these personal and professional development concepts to their staff or volunteer board of directors.

I saw the potential application of a strengths approach everywhere I looked. In this crazy negative world, it felt like a beacon of light, of hope. I was hungry for it, and I had to know more. I decided that I would explore becoming a Gallup-Certified Strengths Coach. Although I was full of passion for the strengths approach, I struggled with the decision to go through the certification process. I almost did not enroll in the course because of the emphasis on coaching. My background was in training, facilitating, and consulting. I just didn't see myself as a coach. I had been recruited by coaching groups over the years by former colleagues who encouraged me to choose this career path. Once again, as I look back, others saw talents in me that I did not see in myself.

It took me a year to take that leap of faith, to invest in myself, in my education. I asked a valued friend whether she thought I should go through the training. She was a practical soul and asked: "Can you afford it? Can you make your money back?" I didn't know, and honestly didn't care. I waited for her lecture. Instead, I received encouragement. She said, "I haven't seen you this excited about anything in years. Go for it!" So off I went to discover my new path with the support of my dear friend. One year later, I became a Gallup-Certified Strengths Coach. It's been the best investment I've ever made!

Fortunately, the required coaching practicum for certification introduced me to the coaching process. My own CliftonStrengths® results helped me identify the value I brought to a coaching relationship. My experience as a facilitator prepared me well for asking good questions and listening to the deeper meaning in my clients' responses. Again, another door opened because of what others could see in me that I initially could not see in myself.

As I developed my strengths, I learned that many of my natural talents served me very well in coaching. My Communication® talent is strong, and I have always been a good listener. Pairing that with my Strategic® talent theme helps me guide my clients in the identification of options and the selection of clear pathways. My strong Relator® and Woo® talents help me quickly build an environment of trust and safety.

I continue to learn and grow every day in this strengths journey. I have discovered that I NEED people. My talents demand that I surround myself with the activity and noise of diverse people and the comfort and joy of those closest to me. I now understand the waves of loneliness I sometimes experience. I also understand why I prefer to work in the library, surrounded by strangers, than alone in my quiet home. People are my oxygen.

My personal strengths journey has helped me better navigate difficult relationships, heal old wounds, forgive and seek forgiveness. I now understand that my lesser talent theme of Discipline® is not likely to come to my rescue when I have a looming deadline, but I have other talents that will! Knowing my full talent profile has been significant in my personal and professional development.

About a week after the completion of my Accelerated coaching class I had a coaching session with a Gallup® Strengths coach. My coach asked me if I knew what I wanted to do with my certification – did I know my preferred niche? Did I have a target market in mind? I remember so clearly my response: "Honestly, I just want to be a cheerleader for the strengths movement! I want to be able to expose as many people as possible to the joy of knowing the uniqueness and the power of their natural talents."

I have also learned that my joy comes from the discovery phase of the strengths journey. I love those immediate reactions and the joy of hearing "Ah, so that's why I do that!" Or, "Now I get why she makes me crazy!" My talent of Activator® loves to initiate the journey to self-awareness. For me, there is nothing more energizing, more fulfilling than serving as a catalyst for that beautiful light bulb moment when the pieces fall in place, and someone awakens to their true potential. This is the start of transformation. I am not trying to change the world. I simply want to touch a life, bring some joy and help others recognize their God-given value.

The Power of Transformation
One of my most powerful coaching experiences was with someone very close to me. It taught me about the true value of CliftonStrengths® and its power to transform. It further validated the leap of faith I took to become a coach.

My oldest granddaughter, Ada, took the StrengthsExplorer® assessment when she was nine years old. This assessment is for younger children and helps parents and others begin to spot talents in their youngsters. I sat next to her as she read the questions and thoughtfully responded. The look on her face when her beautiful talents were revealed warmed my heart. Her sweet face glowed when we talked about how she demonstrated her Caring® talent by volunteering at the Humane Society. She also recognized that her Presence® talent helped her when she made presentations at school. This new self-awareness gave her the confidence to try out for a community play. She also started teaching younger children about pet care. How exciting to see her immediately find new ways to put her talents into action!

After we talked about her talents, she asked me to explain what I did as a strengths coach. I shared that I help people discover their greatest potential and help them achieve their goals and live their lives joyfully and confidently.

When I finished my brief explanation, she looked at me, smiled, and said: "So Grammy, you just drive around and tell people how great they are?" Yes, my dear Ada, that is exactly what I do!

Being Enough

Another profound moment in coaching came when I was working with a highly experienced senior executive and the leadership team of her organization. I had the opportunity to have two coaching sessions with her in addition to the team workshops. She was feeling frustrated and underutilized. Her talent theme of Input® had collected resources to share, yet others did not appear to want them. In addition, her talent theme of Achiever® was frustrated because she was seeking to accomplish some tasks outside of her division. Getting to the root of her challenges was critical to moving her forward.

Before our coaching sessions, she couldn't see the talents she brought to the organization. It was clearly impacting her relationships at work and her personal and professional satisfaction. How could she identify new ways to share resources within her current role? It was important to help her recognize the value she brought to her position and her contributions to the team. Through coaching, she was able to celebrate her own achievements. It had an immediate positive effect on her relationships, and led her to a greater sense of contentment and confidence.

At the close of our last session together, I asked her what she would remember from our coaching experience. After a pause, she looked up at me, tears in her eyes and said, "I have learned that I am enough. I am enough."

That moment of deep, personal transformation, the acknowledgement of true self-worth, that is enough for me! It is a blessing to stand with someone as they grasp the real understanding of their innate value. My purpose as a coach is to ignite the pure joy that comes with the acknowledgement and appreciation of the beautiful gifts with which one has been endowed.

About the Author

Donna M. Gardner, M.A.

Strategic®, Activator®, Woo®, Ideation®, Relator®

Donna M. Gardner is a strengths-focused leadership consultant, facilitator, trainer and coach. A passionate strengths champion, Donna applies her strong relationship building talents and engaging personal style to build and maintain an environment of confidence and trust. She activates her strategic thinking talents and facilitation skills to assist individuals and organizations with goal setting, decision-making and relationship building. Donna connects with her clients with deep commitment and enthusiasm, identifying and building on individual and organizational strengths to enhance performance, increase engagement and improve well-being.

Donna holds a Master's Degree in Communication and is a Gallup-Certified Strengths Coach and a Certified Visioning Facilitator.

You can reach Donna at:

Website: www.donnamgardner.com
Email: Donnamgardner@gmail.com
LinkedIn: linkedin.com/in/donnamgardner

Chapter Ten - Pia Jansson

CONNECTING PEOPLE TO POSSIBILITIES

I have spent a lifetime advising and coaching. It started as a kid, being the go-to person for advice, and then continued throughout my life, both with friends and people at work. Professionally, I ended up starting out as a nurse on a whim, giving up my dream of being an interior designer after a hospital stay. After leaving nursing, I worked as a mail carrier and with people in need of debt consolidation, and then I entered the dental implant field where I have been for almost 30 years in a variety of positions.

During these years, I explored life, and with that, a variety of transformational modalities, many of which I found myself coaching and facilitating in one way or another. As the years went by, I started recognizing similarities between all the different teachings and modalities with my CliftonStrengths® talent of Strategic®.

As I kept looking for new areas to explore that fit my focus, I noticed that the core was often very similar, just using different contexts. They were all such gifts and part of both my journey and who I am today, so I define myself as a "mix n' match" person who has a little bit of everything in my toolbox.

My introduction to CliftonStrengths® began in 2004 through completing the initial assessment. It blew my mind! Not only did

I get present to how powerful I was, or had the potential to be, I also got present to the gap.

It was a chaotic time in the corporation I worked in. At the time of the assessment, I quickly identified why I had been feeling so bad and stressed out. With Relator® as one of my dominant talents, along with Achiever®, Responsibility®, Maximizer® and Activator®, at the time, my entire being was conflicted.

People were being terminated or quitting weekly. Those of us that were still there picked up the slack and morale as a whole at the company was at an all-time low. Many of us had been with the company for years. For many of us it was our life, and during this time people were not being valued, and experienced people were seen as expendable.

I was waiting for my green card at the time, and within six months, once I received it, I was able to leave! Removing myself from that toxic environment nurtured my being. My Activator® talent was finally able to act. Freedom at last! I didn't do anything more with the results, other than take it to heart, heal, and continue exploring different transformational modalities. Coaching continued to be a central part of my life.

Power of Assessments

I took the CliftonStrengths® assessment three times unknowingly. In all cases, my results were similar. Wow! What a wake-up call. In 2016, I was ready to actually digest the information on a different level. I opened up my full talent profile and I saw that all previous talent themes were still dominant. I finally saw myself for who I am. Given my history with transformational work and all the changes I had made in my life since 2004, being more aware of myself than ever, well, that only strengthened the credibility of this assessment for me, and how indeed, it's all about our wiring independent of growth and circumstances.

As I read my Gallup® Strengths Insight Report, I took a step back to take in what the report stated objectively. I got present to what a powerful woman I am and how it was time to do something about it! Looking at my history of advising and coaching in all the roles I've been in throughout my life, I saw how naturally wired I am to coach. I was finally ready to take the leap, claim it and became a Gallup-Certified Strengths Coach in July of 2016.

In July of 2017, I completed the Gallup BP10™ course. The BP10™, also known as the Builder Profile 10, which measures our unique business building talents. For me, that added a whole new dimension to what I've done professionally to date, as I've spent most of my life in the entrepreneurial business realm as an intrapreneur.

One of the keys, from my perspective, is that we don't see our greatness. It's often hidden in the blind spot, and we don't necessarily know what to do with it even after discovering it. Imagine having access to where your entrepreneurial talents are at a young age. If I had access to this when I was in my 20s, it would have saved me years of searching!

I am passionate about the BP10™ because it will save people so much time in building a business. It will help them know how to partner with people who are strong where they are not. To learn the power of delegation so people can thrive where it is a joy for them can also be a relief, a win-win in action and empowerment, each person contributing their best to impact the whole world. Add your unique CliftonStrengths® talents and you'll have the tools you need to build something unique to you. How empowering would it be and what kind of world would that create?

When you read your Strengths Insight Report from the Gallup Strengths Center, you will get present to your greatest potential. Everyone I've coached or spoken with so far all say, "Yep, that's so me," after reading it. You'll also discover the gaps of what could be keeping you from reaching your greatest potential.

A strengths coach can stand in the gap and act as a bridge for you. It's so much faster to have a coach guide you in the process of stepping into your greatness and owning it fully. Walking people through this process and seeing the confidence, engagement, and gratitude for who they are, is amazing to witness! I love sharing the epiphany of why people don't always "get" us. It's a process to embrace your greatness.

I've found that you can shift someone's life and experience of themselves quickly. With a working knowledge of the strengths tools you can move forward in anything that you do! Of course, to sustain change, you need to use the tools and be in action.

Growth is a Journey

Nothing makes me happier than to see people understanding themselves and stepping into their power. Our entire being shifts when we own who we are, play full out and stop making excuses for who we are. It's how we're wired after all, so why not be ourselves?

To me, growth is a journey that will continue until the day I stop breathing. My desire is to be myself, grow, learn new things, expand and step into more of my potential. There are so many possibilities available to us all! When you're being yourself, you inspire others to own every part of their being. Now, wouldn't that be a fun game to play? Instead of pretending to be someone you are not?

What I've always known to be true for me on an energetic level, I now have a language that is in alignment with my inner guidance. From the insights of this assessment, I was able to use this newfound knowledge of myself to create the core of my personal brand.

What I offer as a coach is to help others tap into and trust their own inner guidance as well. To me, the strengths conversation is a natural one for which I'm wired. It's empowering and works great with the other tools that I have in my toolbox. I have a deeper understanding of my needs and a new appreciation for people that have the talents that I don't have. I can now tap into their talents on a whole new level. As I encourage and inspire others to explore what they know, be more of who they uniquely are, it does the same for me.

We all get to expand who we are as beings and with that, step more into our strengths. My Positivity® talent loves to play in this way! Life can be made so easy when guiding people to do what comes so naturally for them.

It always starts and ends with you. When you know what you bring, you'll have a better understanding of the people around you, including talents to look out for when hiring people and building a business. Of every tool I've explored to-date, I've found the topic of Clifton-Strengths® to be a conversation that people can digest easily, while also blending with their life, practices, and beliefs.

Discovering Infinite Possibilities

I play with energy too. Energy is the space that is present between people and within. It's the non-verbal language that is all around us. Asking questions and tapping into what's true for each person and, more importantly,including yourself in the equation. I'm wired for asking questions, which is not always appreciated. I crave what some people consider "out there" conversations. To me, they are simply pragmatic and natural.

When I was introduced to the tools of Access Consciousness®, I found a language for the awareness I had gained (Access Consciousness, 2018). I learned to ask open-ended questions that can change anything. The key is to not answer the question, but rather allow the energy to contribute to new awareness and action. Using these tools and my own awareness, coupled with the inquiries from the CliftonStrengths® materials, is fun and natural to me. Playing outside of the box with its infinite possibilities is what I thrive on. Being "in" the question, rather than the conclusion, is a journey for the energies that are always present for those seeking expanded awareness.

For me, there are no limits to what can be explored in a conversation. Depending on what your unique mix of talents are, we'll explore what your needs are and what topics to explore. There will always be people around us that resist change or who do not seek to be more of themselves. So, are you willing to be in allowance of that while creating a life that you love? What if you following what's true to you can inspire others to do the same? Are you ready to step into who you are no matter who you have around you?

Your Personal Power Statement

According to Gallup® studies, the chances of someone else having your Top 5 talents in the same order is 1 in 33 million (Rath, *StrengthsFinder 2.0*, 2007). Wow! You are, in a sense, your own product and brand. When you start to understand how unique you are, a tagline for your business or a personal power statement suddenly becomes more than just words.

I've worked with salespeople for many years, and when coaching them, I find that a personal power statement helps each person stand out from the competition. Using your dominant talents themes, crafting a statement about who you are and what you bring to the world can be very empowering. This can then be expanded to a team, a company, a state, and even a country.

I add in some other exercises that help my clients discover why they do what they do. We also work on how to apply their talents powerfully into their lives. The awareness of these may impact what you're doing, and you may very well want to make changes as a result.

It's powerful when you focus on people's greatness and what they provide, instead of what's missing. What if we all had access to our unique wiring, and knew how special that was? What kind of conversations would that create? It starts with one person expressing a new perspective and igniting a new conversation. And that conversation could then spread like wildfire and spark new conversations in a group, on a team, in the whole world. Why not allow consciousness to go viral? What an amazing world we could create if we focused on that!

Once my client has a personal power statement, we then set about to create a visual representation. As they look for images to express each talent theme, they will then put that together in a collage. This collage can offer another reinforcement of their uniqueness and what they want to contribute to the world.

Here's what I discovered about myself during this exercise: I was pinning pictures to Pinterest one morning, and I started looking at the mood of the images I chose. I quickly saw patterns as I was focusing on nature pictures. Most, if not all, had images with the sun bursting through. The pictures I kept choosing illustrated a silver lining and hope to me, and I was once again reminded how much the sun drives me, and always has. I've even had a fascination with both sunrises and sunsets since childhood. For me, the sunrise represents the future and hope that sparks my CliftonStrengths® talent of Positivity® and Futuristic®. Sunsets offer peace and stillness that nurtures my Adaptability® talent.

What images are you drawn to? Do you find yourself attracted to different moods depending on how you feel? What images uplift or motivate you?

Many of us spend so much time focusing on what's wrong with us. And it's not always because we were "wrong," but rather we offered a different perspective, a new awareness, that wasn't received by others. What if you could break free from the programming of right and wrong and other people's points of view? What if you could allow others to have their interesting point of view and still continue to create whatever you are creating?

While the strengths movement is about focusing on what's "right" about you, to me, it's really about what's TRUE about you. Shedding the stories of limitations and seeing the gift you are in this world creates infinite possibilities. When you start focusing on what's true about you and not have any judgment about who you are and how you're wired, you embrace your past as a gift in action. Confidence, happiness and productivity often follow.

Transformation Through Strengths

Once, I worked with individuals on a team within an organization. After coaching each of them for several sessions, they made some amazing discoveries. One member had a habit of pointing out what people did wrong. His CliftonStrengths® talent of Analytical® made him critical and demanding of perfection until he became aware. After coaching, he was able to see himself in light of others and he recognized that he had a talent that could guide people into greater understanding. We found a way for him to refocus his talents into a more productive use that served him and others.

Another member of the team made discoveries that impacted his entire life. After a rough year, he took back his personal power, now knowing his uniqueness. His entire world changed when he acknowledged to himself how he was reaching his children in energetic ways. He learned that his Relator® talent, coupled with energy awareness, allowed him to intuitively communicate with his children in different ways. This helped them to hear him. He really understood how much people needed his energy and how he could tap into this as a resource. He is now a happy man! He's so energized that people often tell him they "want what he has," which is the ultimate sign of you being yourself.

A third member of the team was struggling with insecurity and comparison. What he discovered during our coaching sessions was his CliftonStrengths® talent of Competition® getting in the way. He was always comparing himself and coming up lacking. I was able to help him create a new image for himself and embrace how he is wired. We just flipped his perspective of who he is and now, he is confident and a pleasure to be around.

Being part of transformations like this are such gifts to me! It nurtures all my top strengths to be a guide that helps people and businesses step into and build a life based on their talents and what they love.

Appreciation

The possibilities of what can be created with knowing, embracing, and incorporating strengths into your life are endless. It reaches the core of your being and in a quick way and accesses your power. Each journey is different, yet there is a common language available that provides the foundation for discovery and expanded awareness. This allows you to have greater appreciation for who people are without typecasting them.

With strengths, I've found that even people that normally don't express interest in personal growth, are interested to learn more. It's a confirmation about how they view the world. People can be inspired by who they are and what they bring to this world. And then, take aligned action.

We only have this one planet to sustain us at this time, so taking care of it could also be to step into your greatness. What kind of world would we create if we stopped withholding who we truly are and invited others to do the same? What if the strengths movement opened doors where people are otherwise resistant? Are you ready to explore what the strengths movement can do for you in your life?

About the Author

Pia Jansson

Strategic®, Positivity®, Maximizer®, Futuristic®, Activator®

Pia Jansson is a coach for successful men & women who feel like they've lost their mojo in business or life.

She's spent 30 years helping build and reorganize businesses, including areas such as marketing, sales, and education, while also functioning as a strategic partner and executive coach.

She believes that a business is only as strong as its people and helping people step into their best selves is a win-win for everyone involved resulting in a thriving business with engaged employees.

She's a Gallup-Certified Strengths Coach + BP10™ trained, Strategic Partner, Access Bars® Practitioner, Photographer, Author, Lover of life, and more.

You can reach Pia at:

Website: https://piajansson.me
Email: pia@piajansson.me
LinkedIn: https://www.linkedin.com/in/piajansson/

Chapter Eleven - Ken Barr Jr.

EXCEPTIONAL TALENTS

It all came together very quickly. I had recently graduated from my counseling psychology program, completed my internship, and was working as a career counselor/success coach at a community college in Michigan. Within the first four weeks on the job, I received one of the best assignments of my life – to find out everything I could about StrengthsQuest®. StrengthsQuest® (now CliftonStrengths® for Students) is the strengths interface explicitly designed for student success. It uses the same CliftonStrengths® assessment, but its resources are customized for high school and college-age students. It makes complete sense now why this was such a fantastic assignment, as I would soon discover my Top 5: Input®, Maximizer®, Arranger®, Woo®, and Learner®. Why was this job so engaging?

Input® – I love to collect and archive all kinds of information. I took the assessment, read the entire StrengthsQuest® book, and read every report, action item, tool, and resource on the StrengthsQuest® website. And then I read *StrengthsFinder 2.0* by Tom Rath cover to cover.

Maximizer® - I see the strengths in others. A strengths-based approach is how someone with Maximizer® talents naturally sees the world. This approach has always seemed the most intuitive to me. I love this perspective!

Arranger® - I discovered I have a flexible way of coordinating tasks and people. I read about strengths in between counseling appointments. I met with employers who were using strengths in their organizations.

I arranged to have a pilot group of 75 students take the assessment.

Woo® - I enjoy meeting new people and winning them over. I reached out to people all over the US and Canada to find out more about their experiences with strengths. I thoroughly enjoyed speaking with each of them and eagerly added them to my new "strengths network."

Learner® - I love the process of learning. Learning is fun for me. I quickly learned the language of strengths and added appreciative inquiry to my counseling and coaching tools.

Answer: This assignment was especially engaging because I had the opportunity to use my most exceptional talents. The task of researching strengths engaged all of my dominant talents!

Strengths Drives Engagement

This is a lesson that I learned very early on and have shared with all of my clients ever since. My initial reaction to my results mirrored what I have seen repeatedly with thousands of clients - I felt that some of the descriptors were spot on, and I wasn't so sure about some of the others. Input® was the easiest to see. I have been collecting information (and more) since I was a baby! I still have books from elementary school and college, and to me, one of the greatest inventions of all time is undoubtedly the Internet! Learner® seemed to be just as easy to see. I always loved school and often thought the best job ever would be "professional student."

I liked some of the elements described in Maximizer®, but the word "discriminating" made me feel uncomfortable and I thought that it didn't describe me. I would later learn that I most certainly was attracted to highly talented people and that other themes in my Top 10 (Positivity®, Developer®, Relator®, and Includer®) made me quite inclusive.

It took some feedback from my friends and colleagues to understand what Woo® meant for me. When I first read the description, I thought to myself, "this sounds like I'm a used car salesman." Then a friend said to me in a hilarious way that I was a salesman; that I did have the ability to influence people and get folks excited about trying something. He said that what I am selling is their ability to be successful. It wasn't about me; it was about them. Now I could see it! It was easy for me to win others over because I took such a sincere interest in learning about them and helping them accomplish their goals. Who doesn't like that guy?

Arranger® to me was an invisible theme. I didn't necessarily think about the way that I organized and coordinated things. It comes so quickly to me that it feels like I'm not thinking about it at all. I didn't necessarily see it as unique or special. But something cool happened after I read the description and I started to observe the way that I got things done. I realized that it was all very intentional and incredibly strategic! Time, money, personnel, resources, space – all of these factors are being continuously considered to create the best outcomes (high performance and efficiency). Now I had a way to communicate this strength to other people in my life, including co-workers, family, and friends.

The intentional observation of my Arranger® talent made me recognize that I had a knack for putting people in positions to utilize their gifts. I began to notice how useful I had been in my other jobs when I received the opportunity to "tweak" positions. What this looked like on the job was to have the flexibility to move staff members between departments or to adapt job requirements. During my career in hospitality management, I distinctly recall a middle-aged house-keeping houseman who often lagged behind on first shift at a large hotel. He worked at a slower pace, and this would sometimes cause friction with his other teammates who depended on him to change and replenish bed linens. My Maximizer® theme did recognize that while he was not very fast, he was very detail-oriented. This is where my Arranger® theme decided to make a move. I approached him about becoming a second shift houseman, one who would be primarily responsible for turndown service and afternoon service requests. This movement empowered him to deliver his detail-oriented service at a more comfortable pace. It was a complete win-win situation. He was much happier in this role, and the hotel guests appreciated his delivery of high-level customer service.

Early on in my counseling and coaching career (shortly after taking the assessment and having words to describe my themes), I found myself actively volunteering these talents. I focused on developing my Arranger® theme by gaining more and more experience creating and managing events. This was something that I had minimal experience with, but I was attracted to it, and I believed that I could contribute in a novel way. I started small, organizing a couple of practice interview events for students. It began with the recruitment of local employers to give feedback to students during the practice interviews. Each employer worked in our two most popular programs; business and graphic arts. Next, we needed students, which meant the recruitment of influential faculty that taught business communication and visual arts. If the faculty endorses your program and commits time to it, it is guaranteed to have high student participation. I sweetened the deal by promising to facilitate a presentation to each class on the fundamentals of interviewing. In addition, I secured a mini-grant to buy and distribute a padfolio to every student who participated in the interview.

The last thing to do was temporarily convert the first floor of our building into a lobby, reception area, and interview rooms. The event was a win-win. Students received valuable feedback that was developmental, and in an environment that resembled what they would see when they started to apply for jobs in their field. Employers were able to give back to their community in a unique and important way. And while it wasn't the objective of the event, a few students received job offers! This was nearly all done by repositioning and coordinating existing resources - arranging!

The success of the practice interview events energized me and catalyzed the creation of more events on campus. These included lunch and learn discussions centered on strengths, career, and leadership topics. Each event provided additional information and experience that would help me build the next one. I was able to improve promotion and communications using social and traditional media, closed-circuit TV, class visits, and word of mouth. This led to more events, now more prominent and with more moving pieces. Arranging an excellent Dress for Success event was particularly engaging, as it involved a fashion show, custom music, a guest lecturer, and full-salon makeovers. Maximizer® and Woo® talents were drawn on to help ramp up the number and value of giveaways, making this a must-attend event where we were able to dole out more than $1,000 in prizes!

Event design and implementation are now entirely in my wheelhouse. I consider these strengths and am frequently asked to contribute in this area. Developing my Arranger® talents helped lead me to co-create and host the Strengths Learning Intensive, a first of its kind strengths learning event attended by 150+ practitioners from across the USA. Further development of these talents led to my invitation to co-chair the American College Personnel Association (ACPA) - Michigan Annual Conference, a learning event for student affairs practitioners. We were successful in creating a learning event that attendees stated had a "wow" factor while operating on a very modest budget. We reduced costs by securing sponsorships and condensing the event from 2.5 days to 2 days. In fact, we turned the conference from a loss maker to a revenue generator. Amazing what a little "tweaking" can do!

Coaching
Information. Encouragement. Action.

These three words summarize both why I was called to coach and my coaching style. Ever since I was a little kid, I believed that people had the opportunity to change their lives for the better if they had access to information, received encouragement, and could make things actionable. The combination (or degree) of these elements looks different for everyone, but I hold firm that they are necessary to enact positive change.

Coincidently, I have always loved to give people information that is helpful to them. My Input®, Learner®, and Intellection® themes fuel this passion. Furthermore, it has always been my nature to be generous with encouragement. The Relationship Building and Influencing themes of Maximizer®, Woo®, Positivity®, Developer®, Relator®, Includer®, and Empathy® work together to provide authentic support and care (Rath & Conchie, 2008). Lastly, I always look to help find a way to make goals actionable. Arranger®, Learner®, Strategic®, and Intellection® are continually thinking about the best way to make it happen. Therefore, coaching became the mechanism where I could help lots of people and be the best me that I can be.

One of my absolute favorite coaching relationships is the one that I have with a young woman named Tina. I first met Tina when she moved to Michigan to help care for an ailing grandparent. She had a very tough upbringing and had recently been in some serious trouble. Her move was also a way for her to start fresh, enrolling for classes at the local community college. Her dominant talents are as follows: Woo®, Connectedness®, Communication®, Empathy®, and Arranger®.

When Tina and I first met to discuss her strengths, we quickly established rapport, and we both felt very comfortable with one another. She was very warm, enthusiastic, and had a great sense of humor. She was an engaging conversationalist, and she was candid about her life experiences. When discussing people who were less fortunate, she revealed a sensitive side and expressed genuine concern that was very touching. She possessed a passion for helping others and wanted to make a difference.

What surprised me during that first coaching conversation was that while Tina demonstrated strong Relationship Building and Influencing talents, she did not readily see these things in herself (Rath & Conchie, 2008). Her body language shifted, showing discomfort, and her voice changed to express doubt in her talents. When speaking about herself, Tina would make a statement as if she were asking a question. She did not think that her combination of talents was especially unique.

I knew what I needed to do. I needed to use my Maximizer® and Woo® talents to "hold up the mirror." What Tina needed from me in that meeting was to help her see the incredible gifts that she possessed. Tina expressed to me that her career goal was to be a social worker. So I asked her some of the things that social workers do. She easily explained to me that they help individuals and families cope with and solve their problems. She told me that they help people get connected to resources and services. I listened to her and then I calmly reflected back to her all of the instances that she had described to me where she had done these things for friends, family members, and other students. I reminded her that I had personally seen her walk students to get connected with campus success services. What type of student does that? I let her sit with that for a moment. Her body language showed me that now she could see these talents. Then I said to her, "Tina, you already are a social worker." She smiled and said, "Yeah, I guess I am."

We started our coaching relationship with encouragement. Next, we would focus on information. Specifically, we focused on what she needed to learn to transfer to a four-year school. Being a first-generation college student had limited Tina's access to "college knowledge," information that is helpful for navigating complex processes and environments. During our coaching conversations, we talked about what her goals were and what talents she would employ to make progress toward those goals. To be successful, Tina would leverage her Woo® and Communication® talents to build relationships on campus. She was a natural networker, making appointments with her advisors and seeking out faculty for assistance when she needed it. Acquiring information was most engaging to Tina when it was a relational process. This was a significant discovery. She used this knowledge to help herself and she kept helping other students. She would often get students connected to campus success services by talking about how helpful they were to her.

When it came to making things actionable, Tina had no shortage of ideas. Using her Arranger® talents, she could quickly think of ways to make things happen. The challenge was her believing that it was a good idea. Sometimes she would come to me and ask me if I thought something would work. I would ask her for details, and usually she would have great strategies. This happened so frequently that I soon began to repeat myself: "Trust your instincts."

I am very proud to say that Tina got her Associate's degree, then her Bachelor's degree, and then her Master's degree! In fact, she was awarded the Presidential Scholar Award for the school of social work. This award is the highest academic honor bestowed upon an under-graduate student. Only one student is selected from the entire class of social work students. Sure enough, she is officially a social worker, currently helping youth that are homeless or in crisis. The talent was always there. My job as a coach was to help her see it.

Possibilities

Why should we take a strengths-based approach?

I hear this question so frequently that I almost reflexively respond "why shouldn't we take a strengths-based approach?" Consider the possibilities if everyone was committed to identifying, cultivating, and utilizing their unique gifts.

Consider the difference it would make in our closest relationships if we were intentional about focusing on what is right with our significant other. Imagine how you would feel if your partner appreciated your unique perspective and supported what you needed to be your best self. How would they think if you did the same? Imagine the decrease in conflict if we understood the motivations behind our thoughts, feelings, and behaviors.

Consider the possibilities the world of work would present, if everyone knew their greatest strengths. Think about how liberating it would be to pursue roles that would fully engage your talents. Can you picture a workforce emboldened with the confidence that comes with delivering amazing outcomes time and time again? Can you see the potential for intentional team blending? What if your supervisor created a development plan for you that specifically added knowledge and skills to your identified talents?

What would schools look like if they took a strengths-based approach? How do you think students would respond to learning experiences that helped them identify their innate talents? What if schools and teachers were given the autonomy to allow students to select specific areas where they would like to dedicate additional time to strength-building? How quickly could we create experiences that draw out the very best in our students? Would school be more engaging? Would it be more (gasp) fun?

Think about the global implications of seeing the very best in others. What if the world shared a universal language that described what is right about people? Would it increase trust? Would it change our mindset to see differences as an advantage? Could it minimize conflict? Imagine the near endless potential for working together to help solve our most significant challenges.

Why should we take a strengths-based approach? Perhaps the most straightforward reasons are that it feels right and it works. The analytics show us what happens when individuals and organizations focus on their strengths; they enjoy a higher quality of life, and they experience more favorable outcomes. Millions have already experienced the positive effects of discovering their strengths. Imagine what the world will look like when billions of people discover their natural gifts.

These possibilities excite me! I'm committed. I've been doing it this way so long, that it is hard for me to imagine not taking a strengths-based approach. I've dedicated my life to helping people become the very best that they can be. I have experienced a multitude of benefits by personally going through a strengths discovery process, and I've helped thousands more make progress on that journey from awareness to application. I like to think of it as a beacon of leadership. It has, without a doubt, been one of the most rewarding things I have ever undertaken.

Now it's your turn. You're reading a coaching book for a reason. Will you join me? What commitments will you make to advance the strengths movement?

About the Author

Ken Barr Jr.

Input®, Maximizer®, Arranger®, Woo®, Learner®

Ken is a Licensed Professional Counselor, career coach, and organizational consultant dedicated to helping individuals and teams discover, develop, and apply their strengths. He was Michigan's first Gallup-Certified Strengths Coach.

Ken works frequently in the education, non-profit, retail, hospitality, healthcare, and customer service fields providing solutions that include program startup, team development, best practices, recognition, and talent insights.

Ken has been part of the strengths movement for more than 11 years and has helped more than 14,000 people begin their strengths journey.

You can reach Ken at:

Website: beaconleadershipllc.com
Email: KenBarrJr@gmail.com

Chapter Twelve - Debby Rauch Lissaur, CPCC

UNDERSTANDING COLLEAGUES & ACCELERATING PERFORMANCE

A seven-year-old girl was waiting in a two-hour line at the World's Fair Czech Pavilion with her parents and sister. Standing in one spot was unbearable. She noticed a basement office window in the building next to where they stood. She and her sister went to investigate.

"Mommy, go to the front of the line," she exclaimed. But her mother explained they needed to wait. "No, Mommy, the nice lady in that window I met down there told us to meet her at the front of the line, and she'd let us in." And just like that, we zoomed right into the exhibit.

This is my earliest memory of using one of my strongest CliftonStrengths® talents, Woo® (Winning others over). I've loved meeting new people as long as I can remember, making connections that happen in an instant. I love to connect to all different people wherever I go - at networking events, baseball games, the airport. I truly delight in meeting new people and hearing their stories. The connections are real but fleeting. And that's okay, because I couldn't possibly "keep" all the people I meet. Some have become lifelong friends, but most are happy memories of "drive-by" interactions. In my corporate life, I put interview candidates immediately at ease, allowing me to see their real selves, for good and for bad, and my Woo® talent contributes to the immediate bond that forms between my clients and me.

I use CliftonStrengths® as a foundation in my calling as an executive strengths-based coach, leadership development facilitator, and in my life in general. I believe strengths awareness builds confidence, elevates engagement and brings people together.

Every day we go to work and see a lot of the same people. Odds are, except for a few connections that organically form, we have little more than a military understanding of colleagues: Name, Rank, Serial Number. It might sound something like, "Sarah is a brand manager in Marketing and does brand positioning. Marlene is a supervisor who works in Accounting; she sends out invoices. Elisa is a systems analyst in IT. She does tech stuff."

Unlocking the Secret "People Code"

What if you went beyond titles and essential functions to understand someone's natural talents? What if you knew Sarah spent her free time networking at her local business club, exchanging ideas with different women? Might she identify potential new business leads for your company?

What if you knew Marlene had a super organized filing system, cataloging every business proposal the firm created in the last 15 years, while the rest of her department was pure chaos? Might she help systematize the entire team?

What if you knew that Elisa loved to pontificate for hours on possible home improvement apps — might she have engaging automation ideas for you?

The above scenarios describe what happens when you go beyond Name, Rank, & Serial Number, and lean into CliftonStrengths®. Each of these employees has unique gifts and talents that can be discovered through the assessment. Once you know how people's talent themes stack up, it's like having a secret code to understanding how to inspire and engage them, while maximizing the performance of that individual or team. When you leverage what people already love to do and let them apply those talents every day at work, they are statistically more likely to be engaged, productive, and happy!

Stumbling Upon the World of Strengths

Before I go too much further, let me explain how I came to appreciate the world of CliftonStrengths®.

I've always liked positive psychology, the study and expansion of what's right with people rather than a hard focus on what's wrong with them. Surely, we need to address weaknesses, but it never made sense to me to try to inspire people by fixating on what's wrong them. Who is going to give their best performance after being told 15 reasons why they are not good enough?!

In my work as an executive coach and leadership development facilitator, I noticed the tendency for a lot of assessments to cause a divide between colleagues. They labeled each other, and often became entrenched in judgment, which did not serve them or their teams.

Another thing I noticed was a palpable "lift" when clients touched upon passions, and a similar energy "dive" when talking about areas outside their genius work. It seemed clear that increased awareness around passions was the key to engagement at work and life in general. So, I helped clients get clear on which aspects of work "juiced" them, so they could "dial up" their focus in those areas. We also identified passion-driven causes for which they might volunteer, which, in turn, elevated their energy at work. Most interestingly, while becoming better acquainted with themselves, their tolerance of others' shortcomings and their appreciation of others' talents grew.

Wanting to increase client self-appreciation, I was already using a variety of assessments - lots of them! I've been certified in so many tools that it has become a standing joke. Friends have jokingly forbidden me to get more certifications, but I can not, NOT. I find it so fascinating to "unpack" what makes a person tick.

Even I had to acknowledge my certification basket was sufficiently robust. So, imagine when a client asked if I were certified in CliftonStrengths®, and if not, would I consider it. I was thinking, "I have enough certifications. Surely I can figure out the results of this one on my own."

I happily debriefed the executive I had been hired to coach. I was feeling all proud of myself, but then the organization wanted to do more extensive work with the tool, and it just so happened that Gallup® was offering a certification course in London. The kids were away at camp, and my husband was drowning in work. Solo road trip? Why not? I flew to London, and that training launched a passion so deep within me, I would never be the same.

Keys to Excellence

I loved that CliftonStrengths® seemed to answer the question, "In what do I excel?"

I was surprised at how much depth there was to this tool! What became clear was that each person's innate talents unfolded like a unique thumbprint, with limitless talent combinations. And when everyone literally has a different profile, you can't easily label others. I liked that!

There are 34 possible talent themes, ranked uniquely for each person. The odds of having two employees at a firm with that same 34-theme ranking is practically zero. No matter how big the company. Even a global company with tens of thousands of employees. Astounding!

When I got home, I re-did the CliftonStrengths® debrief with my client, realizing I had so much more to offer, given my newly minted certification. We found exciting ways to apply talents and elevate her performance, and it opened up new doors of communication.

For example, she historically complained to me about a co-worker who "took forever" to get work done, though she admitted the colleague's work was stellar. When she realized that her teammate, who was cautious and meticulous, was high in the talent theme of Deliberative®, we brainstormed on the best way to interact with her. She decided she would give her co-worker extra time when possible. When deadlines were unavoidably tight, she'd let her know, so they could agree upon the most critical areas on which to focus should time run short. Through mutual talent appreciation and improved communication between them, tension dissipated significantly.

The Same Talent: Only Different

Even when people have talent themes in common, those same talents can read like night and day in the Gallup Strengths Insight Report, because other talents are woven in to create this one-of-a-kind, dynamic picture. Talents work together like a secret, behind-the-scenes team. Theme dynamics is what you call this talent blending. Let me give you an example.

In simplistic terms, Strategic® sees the path forward, anticipating any roadblocks along the way, to work around them in order to achieve a given goal, while shifting gears as needed to incorporate new information. It's seeing choices in how to approach a task and instinctively knowing, in your gut, which will translate to success.

Both my colleague and I have Strategic® in our dominant profile. Our Strengths Insight Reports should read the same, right? Actually, they read completely differently because we each have different talent themes woven into that description.

In my description of Strategic®, it describes how I like to be on the cutting edge of my field and generating entirely new ways of seeing or doing things; that I am strong at identifying the core problem at hand and solving it, or strong at turning problems into opportunities. My Ideation®, Input® and Positivity® talents are clearly at play.

My colleague's description highlights her love for note taking (you should see her walls covered in giant sticky notes, outlining her vision). It also reveals that she inspires people to start projects, identify goals and sees opportunity and trends before others. Her Activator®, Achiever®, and Futuristic® talents forcefully push their way in to assist her strategic decision-making.

Same Strategic® theme as mine, yet not. Fascinating!

Theme Dynamics: The Story of Me

Did you know our talent profiles tell a story about us? I'll do my best to paint my story for you, and I challenge you to create your own. I'm taking creative liberty in personifying each of my talents so that you can see how they dynamically "play" together for me.

Since Woo® comes in at the top of the pack, it thinks it's in charge. It's not. So, who is? Developer® (the "teacher" and "champion of others"), along with Includer® (an urgent talent theme that wants everyone to have a seat at the table).

My Woo® collects people. It loves meeting strangers. It feels compelled to talk to everyone. (If, when you walk into an elevator, you get aggravated to discover the person in there is wearing earbuds, so you can't talk to them, you might be high in this talent. If you get aggravated when people like me start talking to you, well, probably Woo® is not in your dominant group. Why be aggravated over earbuds? Because it's a missed opportunity to connect with others! And Woo® is all about wanting that connection.) Woo® literally wants to talk to everyone it sees, everywhere it goes, because people are so fascinating!

Communication® knows just which words or stories to choose to be engaging, while Positivity® adds humor, irreverence, and fun. Together, with Woo®, they form a happy trio, entertaining the masses. However, just because they are high on my list, they are still not in charge. They are just "funnel-fillers" taking orders from Developer® and Includer®, who both insist the top trio get out there and keep collecting people.

Empathy® reads the emotional current of who wants to be included and who is just peacefully hanging out on their own, content in their solitude.

Developer® tirelessly looks to take people under its wing, growing people's leadership, teaching new skills. (It should be noted that Developer® is the one explaining most of what is in this chapter. Developer® wants you to feel smart. Accomplished. Confident.) The more confident people feel, the more they realize their unique contribution and that they belong, which pleases Includer® immensely.

So, there's this dynamic tension between the top trio who are often exhausted, continually collecting people and the desire to acknowledge each individual. This funnel filling results in "people overload." We can't possibly build relationships with this many people! What to do?

Enter Strategic®, which makes sense amid this sea of collected people, assessing the long-term need for each connection. It sees in an instant who just needs a friendly, quick, drive-by chat, who needs perhaps a bit more reassurance, and then, a soft release. It notices who is ready to embark on a leadership transformation, suggesting longer-term support, and who has the potential to be a lifelong friend—because we want to keep some. In its "sorting" role, Strategic® sounds like:

"You three, you're fine. You don't need us. It was truly nice meeting you. You, over there, hang for a bit if you want, but you're ok, too. And you, by the door, you stay by us. We see greatness in you that we don't think you yet see, and we'd like to tell you about it. And last but not least, you, over there, we are keeping you forever as our friend."

Other themes jump in. Individualization® is fascinated by what is unique in those we meet, while Connectedness® is in awe of how, despite these unique qualities, we are, in the end, all the same. Ideation® loves to brainstorm on ways to help others, and Maximizer® can't resist tweaking everything to make it a wee bit better. And so on.

It's a constant dynamic orchestra of interwoven talents that make me …well…me! This is where it really gets fun!

So, what story do your themes paint about you?

Translating English into English
More fascinating than how talents work within one person, is how they serve to improve communication between people.

I once coached two individuals on a team at a communication company: Marion, a high-level director, and one of her junior managers, Cathy. There was tension between them. Marion felt Cathy was a buzz kill. No matter what ideas were generated, Cathy shot them down. Cathy felt the director was irresponsible, continually changing gears all the time, and nothing was getting done. Their communication was poor. Their talent profiles offered a potential explanation for their miscommunication.

Marion, the director, was high in the talent themes of Ideation® and Futuristic® and loved brainstorming and thinking of what might be possible. Marion also had so many dreams of what could be for the company and their customers. She yearned to take their organization to the next level. She felt Cathy was handcuffing her vision, always stating why something wouldn't work.

Cathy, on the other hand, was strong in the talent theme of Context® and used historical references as a filter for decision making. She was also dominant in the talent of Deliberative® and was meticulously thorough and cautious to avoid potential roadblocks. Activator® ranked high for Cathy, too, meaning she was an independent worker who jumped to get things started.

Every time Marion would come into a room and free associate her ideas, Cathy assumed she was supposed to act upon all of them—and the sooner, the better to uncover and avoid all potential problems early. She didn't understand Marion was simply thinking out loud, musing possibilities. Cathy would think about similar past endeavors that were unsuccessful, and she wanted to help Marion, alerting her to these failures so that the director wouldn't run into similar problems. Cathy also warned of potential future problems where things might go wrong, and again, alerted Marion so that the director would not fail.

Unfortunately, Marion just saw Cathy's warnings as negativity, completely misunderstanding Cathy's good intentions. Likewise, Cathy saw the director as a chaos maker, requesting projects which often were abandoned half way through for the next idea. Marion was shocked to learn that Cathy and her team were trying to implement all of Marion's ideas because Marion was just brainstorming. To Marion, each idea fed off of the last, and it was her way of getting to the "real" big idea to realize her vision.

Once Cathy understood Marion's intentions, a lot of pressure was released. They agreed that if Marion wanted an idea to be implemented, she'd explicitly say so. Marion softened when she understood Cathy was simply trying to protect her and their team from failing, by pointing out the historical failures and potential future roadblocks.

There had been a huge communication barrier, and, through the use of CliftonStrengths®, I was able to help translate "English into English," giving them a new common language. Now they understood each other's motives, appreciated each other's gifts, and working together became immeasurably more positive and productive.

Building Trust

Jennifer was a senior executive at a pharmaceutical company. Her boss had recently been hired, and Jennifer and I were in the middle of a long-term coaching engagement. Jennifer's dominant talent profile included the talent of Self-Assurance®. Jennifer was unusual. You could feel her confidence when she walked into a room. She spoke with certainty and to be on her team meant you were well supported. She liked to be independent, having an internal compass guiding her, even amid chaos, and was seemingly unflappable.

Her new boss frequently visited Jennifer's office, asking about projects and wanting status updates. She felt micromanaged and was upset her boss didn't trust her. She and I talked about the situation, and we realized her boss had not stated anything to indicate he didn't trust her. She just assumed it from his frequent visits. She decided to share her concerns, respectfully and directly.

Her boss appreciated her honesty, explaining that whenever he started in a new position, he liked to be "hands on" so he could "feel" the work himself. But after a few weeks, when he got the essence of the workflow, he would back off. He told Jennifer he visited her office more frequently than others because he felt she had a strong command of what was going on and he knew whatever she told him would be solid. He never intended her to read his frequent visits as a lack of confidence in her.

The conversation helped him to better understand the need to give her a sense of independence, knowing that she would ask for help when needed. And he promised her that if he had an issue with her work, he would tell her directly so that if he came to chat, it was exactly that—just a chat.

With the CliftonStrengths® information, we have an opportunity to improve communication and build bridges between people. These bridges ultimately lead to mutual understanding and serve to build trust.

True Diversity

Some define "diversity" as the following: men versus women, the color of one's skin, or restoring dignity to a particular group who is feeling marginalized. Of course, I recognize the need to teach respect for all the sizes and shapes that make up our human palate, and I realize there are facets to particular clusters of like-minded people which can best be addressed as a subgroup.

Something about this type of traditional diversity focus, or at least making it the exclusive answer to diversity training makes me uncomfortable. Yes, it's important to level the playing field or right a wrong. In fact, we must do so.

But, is diversity meant to be a correction of sorts? Or, is it meant to draw from the maximum number of differentiated resources that can possibly be identified, so as to elevate performance? From where I sit, the latter has tremendous, untapped potential.

If we want the type of diversity that will have tremendous impact on the bottom line, it would be ideal if everyone were to bring something different to the table. In order for these differences to be relevant, they would need to provide tangible, easily accessible, and actionable results.

So how can we attain maximum advantage for our organizations and our world? How can we find a diversity diamond with millions of unique and brilliant facets? The answer is a strengths-based focus. Every person has a unique talent profile. No two are the same! Imagine harnessing the power of a vast array of talents! Imagine a world where each person's unique contribution is unearthed, valued, nurtured and celebrated!

This limitless approach exemplifies true diversity.

I challenge you to begin looking through a strengths-based lens. See all the potential inside of you and inside of all those around you, maybe people you had assumed were the same as you, but actually are not. People who perhaps had previously eluded you, suddenly being revealed as a major asset. People who, when working together in a world of mutual appreciation, would create an electric force of possibility. There is so much power just waiting to be harnessed!

Know your strengths. Knowledge is power!

About the Author

Debby Rauch Lissaur, CPCC

Woo®, Communication®, Positivity®, Strategic®, Developer®

Debby Rauch Lissaur is the President & Chief Positivity Instigator at Optimism, Inc., a strengths-based executive coaching & leadership development company dedicated to positivity, personal responsibility & kindness. She was the first Gallup-Certified Strengths Coach in the NY/NJ area, has been a featured guest on the Strengths Activation Show and a guest blogger for Gallup's Called-to-Coach.

She is the proud & passionate Co-Founder of a nine-month experiential women's leadership platform: IgnitedNation@Work™ & IgnitedNation@College™, initiatives designed to empower & inspire women in the corporate and college sectors. Debby most enjoys working with high-energy, professional and college men and women, seeking to take their game up a notch.

You can reach Debby at:

Website: www.OptimismInc.com
Email: Debby@OptimismInc.com

REFERENCES

Access Consciousness, LLC. (2018). Retrieved from https://www.accessconsciousness.com/en/

Buckingham, M., & Clifton, D. O. (2001). Now, Discover Your Strengths. New York City: Simon and Schuster.

Evans, J., & Kelsey, A. (2016). Strengths Based Marriage: Build a Stronger Relationship by Understanding Each Other's Gifts. Nashville: Thomas Nelson.

Lencioni, P. M. (2010). The Five Dysfunctions of a Team: A Leadership Fable. Hoboken, NJ: John Wiley & Sons.

Palmer, P. J. (2015). Let Your Life Speak: Listening for the Voice of Vocation. San Francisco: Jossey-Bass.

Rath, T. (2007). StrengthsFinder 2.0. New York City: Gallup Press.

Rath, T., & Conchie, B. (2008). Strengths Based Leadership: Great Leaders, Teams, and Why People Follow. New York City: Simon and Schuster.

Sinek, S. (2014, March 19). How Leaders Inspire Action. Retrieved from TEDx Talks Puget Sound: https://www.ted.com/talks/simon_sinek_how_great_leaders_inspire_action/transcript?language=en

Winseman, A., Clifton, D. O., & Liesveld, C. (2004). Living Your Strengths. New York City: Simon and Schuster.

APPENDIX

CliftonStrengths® Long Theme Descriptions

Achiever®: Your Achiever theme helps explain your drive. Achiever describes a constant need for achievement. You feel as if every day starts at zero. By the end of the day, you must achieve something tangible in order to feel good about yourself. And by "every day" you mean every single day — workdays, weekends, vacations. No matter how much you may feel you deserve a day of rest, if the day passes without some form of achievement, no matter how small, you will feel dissatisfied. You have an internal fire burning inside you. It pushes you to do more, to achieve more. After each accomplishment is reached, the fire dwindles for a moment, but very soon it rekindles itself, forcing you toward the next accomplishment. Your relentless need for achievement might not be logical. It might not even be focused. But it will always be with you. As an Achiever, you must learn to live with this whisper of discontent. It does have its benefits. It brings you the energy you need to work long hours without burning out. It is the jolt you can always count on to get you started on new tasks, new challenges. It is the power supply that causes you to set the pace and define the levels of productivity for your workgroup. It is the theme that keeps you moving.

Activator®: "When can we start?" This is a recurring question in your life. You are impatient for action. You may concede that analysis has its uses or that debate and discussion can occasionally yield some valuable insights, but deep down you know that only action is real. Only action can make things happen. Only action leads to performance. Once a decision is made, you cannot not act. Others may worry that "there are still some things we don't know," but this doesn't seem to slow you. If the decision has been made to go across town, you know that the fastest way to get there is to go stoplight to stoplight. You are not going to sit around waiting until all the lights have turned green. Besides, in your view, action and thinking are not opposites. In fact, guided by your Activator theme, you believe that action is the best device for learning. You make a decision, you take action, you look at the result, and you learn. This learning informs your next action and your next. How can you grow if you have nothing to react to? Well, you believe you can't. You must put yourself out there. You must take the next step. It is the only way to keep your thinking fresh and informed. The bottom line is this: You know you will be judged not by what you say, not by what you think, but by what you get done. This does not frighten you. It pleases you.

Adaptability®: You live in the moment. You don't see the future as a fixed destination. Instead, you see it as a place that you create out of the choices that you make right now. And so you discover your future one choice at a time. This doesn't mean that you don't have plans. You probably do. But this theme of Adaptability does enable you to respond willingly to the demands of the moment even if they pull you away from your plans. Unlike some, you don't resent sudden requests or unforeseen detours. You expect them. They are inevitable. Indeed, on some level you actually look forward to them. You are, at heart, a very flexible person who can stay productive when the demands of work are pulling you in many different directions at once.

Analytical®: Your Analytical theme challenges other people: "Prove it. Show me why what you are claiming is true." In the face of this kind of questioning, some will find that their brilliant theories wither and die. For you, this is precisely the point. You do not necessarily want to destroy other people's ideas, but you do insist that their theories be sound. You see yourself as objective and dispassionate. You like data because they are value free. They have no agenda. Armed with these data, you search for patterns and connections. You want to understand how certain patterns affect one another. How do they combine? What is their outcome? Does this outcome fit with the theory being offered or the situation being confronted? These are your questions. You peel the layers back until, gradually, the root cause or causes are revealed. Others see you as logical and rigorous. Over time, they will come to you in order to expose someone's "wishful thinking" or "clumsy thinking" to your refining mind. It is hoped that your analysis is never delivered too harshly. Otherwise, others may avoid you when that "wishful thinking" is their own.

Arranger®: You are a conductor. When faced with a complex situation involving many factors, you enjoy managing all of the variables, aligning and realigning them until you are sure you have arranged them in the most productive configuration possible. In your mind, there is nothing special about what you are doing. You are simply trying to figure out the best way to get things done. But others, lacking this theme, will be in awe of your ability. "How can you keep so many things in your head at once?" they will ask. "How can you stay so flexible, so willing to shelve well-laid plans in favor of some brand-new configuration that has just occurred to you?" But you cannot imagine behaving in any other way. You are a shining example of effective flexibility, whether you are changing travel schedules at the last minute because a better fare has popped up or mulling over just the right combination of people and resources to accomplish a new project. From the mundane to the complex, you are always looking for the perfect configuration. Of course, you are at your best in dynamic situations. Confronted with the unexpected, some complain that plans devised with such care cannot be changed, while others take refuge in the existing rules or procedures. You don't do either. Instead, you jump into the confusion, devising new options, hunting for new paths of least resistance and figuring out new partnerships — because, after all, there might just be a better way.

Belief®: If you possess a strong Belief theme, you have certain core values that are enduring. These values vary from one person to another, but ordinarily your Belief theme causes you to be family-oriented, altruistic, even spiritual and to value responsibility and high ethics — both in yourself and others. These core values affect your behavior in many ways. They give your life meaning and satisfaction; in your view, success is more than money and prestige. They provide you with direction, guiding you through the temptations and distractions of life toward a consistent set of priorities. This consistency is the foundation for all your relationships. Your friends call you dependable. "I know where you stand," they say. Your Belief makes you easy to trust. It also demands that you find work that meshes with your values. Your work must be meaningful; it must matter to you. And guided by your Belief theme, it will matter only if it gives you a chance to live out your values.

Command®: Command leads you to take charge. Unlike some people, you feel no discomfort with imposing your views on others. On the contrary, once your opinion is formed, you need to share it with others. Once your goal is set, you feel restless until you have aligned others with you. You are not frightened by confrontation; rather, you know that confrontation is the first step toward resolution. Whereas others may avoid facing up to life's unpleasantness, you feel compelled to present the facts or the truth, no matter how unpleasant it may be. You need things to be clear between people and challenge them to be clear-eyed and honest. You push them to take risks. You may even intimidate them. And while some may resent this, labeling you opinionated, they often willingly hand you the reins. People are drawn toward those who take a stance and ask them to move in a certain direction. Therefore, people will be drawn to you. You have presence. You have Command.

Communication®: You like to explain, to describe, to host, to speak in public and to write. This is your Communication theme at work. Ideas are a dry beginning. Events are static. You feel a need to bring them to life, to energize them, to make them exciting and vivid. And so you turn events into stories and practice telling them. You take the dry idea and enliven it with images and examples and metaphors. You believe that most people have a very short attention span. They are bombarded by information, but very little of it survives. You want your information — whether an idea, an event, a product's features and benefits, a discovery, or a lesson — to survive. You want to divert their attention toward you and then capture it, lock it in. This is what drives your hunt for the perfect phrase. This is what draws you toward dramatic words and powerful word combinations. This is why people like to listen to you. Your word pictures pique their interest, sharpen their world and inspire them to act.

Competition®: Competition is rooted in comparison. When you look at the world, you are instinctively aware of other people's performance. Their performance is the ultimate yardstick. No matter how hard you tried, no matter how worthy your intentions, if you reached your goal but did not outperform your peers, the achievement feels hollow. Like all competitors, you need other people. You need to compare. If you can compare, you can compete, and if you can compete, you can win. And when you win, there is no feeling quite like it. You like measurement because it facilitates comparisons. You like other competitors because they invigorate you. You like contests because they must produce a winner. You particularly like contests where you know you have the inside track to be the winner. Although you are gracious to your fellow competitors and even stoic in defeat, you don't compete for the fun of competing. You compete to win. Over time, you will come to avoid contests where winning seems unlikely.

Connectedness®: Things happen for a reason. You are sure of it. You are sure of it because in your soul you know that we are all connected. Yes, we are individuals, responsible for our own judgments and in possession of our own free will, but nonetheless we are part of something larger. Some may call it the collective unconscious. Others may label it spirit or life force. But whatever your word of choice, you gain confidence from knowing that we are not isolated from one another or from the earth and the life on it. This feeling of Connectedness implies certain responsibilities. If we are all part of a larger picture, then we must not harm others because we will be harming ourselves. We must not exploit because we will be exploiting ourselves. Your awareness of these responsibilities creates your value system. You are considerate, caring and accepting. Certain of the unity of humankind, you are a bridge builder for people of different cultures. Sensitive to the invisible hand, you can give others comfort that there is a purpose beyond our humdrum lives. The exact articles of your faith will depend on your upbringing and your culture, but your faith is strong. It sustains you and your close friends in the face of life's mysteries.

Consistency®: Balance is important to you. You are keenly aware of the need to treat people the same, no matter what their station in life, so you do not want to see the scales tipped too far in any one person's favor. In your view, this leads to selfishness and individualism. It leads to a world where some people gain an unfair advantage because of their connections or their background or their greasing of the wheels. This is truly offensive to you. You see yourself as a guardian against it. In direct contrast to this world of special favors, you believe that people function best in a consistent environment where the rules are clear and are applied to everyone equally. This is an environment where people know what is expected. It is predictable and evenhanded. It is fair. Here each person has an even chance to show his or her worth.

Context®: You look back. You look back because that is where the answers lie. You look back to understand the present. From your vantage point, the present is unstable, a confusing clamor of competing voices. It is only by casting your mind back to an earlier time, a time when the plans were being drawn up, that the present regains its stability. The earlier time was a simpler time. It was a time of blueprints. As you look back, you begin to see these blueprints emerge. You realize what the initial intentions were. These blueprints or intentions have since become so embellished that they are almost unrecognizable, but now this Context theme reveals them again. This understanding brings you confidence. No longer disoriented, you make better decisions because you sense the underlying structure. You become a better partner because you understand how your colleagues came to be who they are. And counterintuitively, you become wiser about the future because you saw its seeds being sown in the past. Faced with new people and new situations, it will take you a little time to orient yourself, but you must give yourself this time. You must discipline yourself to ask the questions and allow the blueprints to emerge because no matter what the situation, if you haven't seen the blueprints, you will have less confidence in your decisions.

Deliberative®: You are careful. You are vigilant. You are a private person. You know that the world is an unpredictable place. Everything may seem in order, but beneath the surface you sense many risks. Rather than denying these risks, you draw each one out into the open. Then each risk can be identified, assessed and ultimately reduced. Thus, you are a fairly serious person who approaches life with a certain reserve. For example, you like to plan ahead so as to anticipate what might go wrong. You select your friends cautiously and keep your own counsel when the conversation turns to personal matters. You are careful not to give too much praise and recognition, lest it be misconstrued. If some people don't like you because you are not as effusive as others, then so be it. For you, life is not a popularity contest. Life is something of a minefield. Others can run through it recklessly if they so choose, but you take a different approach. You identify the dangers, weigh their relative impact and then place your feet deliberately. You walk with care.

Developer®: You see the potential in others. Very often, in fact, potential is all you see. In your view, no individual is fully formed. On the contrary, each individual is a work in progress, alive with possibilities. And you are drawn toward people for this very reason. When you interact with others, your goal is to help them experience success. You look for ways to challenge them. You devise interesting experiences that can stretch them and help them grow. And all the while, you are on the lookout for the signs of growth — a new behavior learned or modified, a slight improvement in a skill, a glimpse of excellence or of "flow" where previously there were only halting steps. For you, these small increments — invisible to some — are clear signs of potential being realized. These signs of growth in others are your fuel. They bring you strength and satisfaction. Over time, many will seek you out for help and encouragement because on some level they know that your helpfulness is both genuine and fulfilling to you.

Discipline®: Your world needs to be predictable. It needs to be ordered and planned. So you instinctively impose structure on your world. You set up routines. You focus on timelines and deadlines. You break long-term projects into a series of specific short-term plans, and you work through each plan diligently. You are not necessarily neat and clean, but you do need precision. Faced with the inherent messiness of life, you want to feel in control. The routines, the timelines, the structure, all of these help create this feeling of control. Lacking this theme of Discipline, others may sometimes resent your need for order, but there need not be conflict. You must understand that not everyone feels your urge for predictability; they have other ways of getting things done. Likewise, you can help them understand and even appreciate your need for structure. Your dislike of surprises, your impatience with errors, your routines and your detail orientation don't need to be misinterpreted as controlling behaviors that box people in. Rather, these behaviors can be understood as your instinctive method for maintaining your progress and your productivity in the face of life's many distractions.

Empathy®: You can sense the emotions of those around you. You can feel what they are feeling as though their feelings are your own. Intuitively, you are able to see the world through their eyes and share their perspective. You do not necessarily agree with each person's perspective. You do not necessarily feel pity for each person's predicament — this would be sympathy, not Empathy. You do not necessarily condone the choices each person makes, but you do understand. This instinctive ability to understand is powerful. You hear the unvoiced questions. You anticipate the need. Where others grapple for words, you seem to find the right words and the right tone. You help people find the right phrases to express their feelings — to themselves as well as to others. You help them give voice to their emotional life. For all these reasons, other people are drawn to you.

Focus®: "Where am I headed?" you ask yourself. You ask this question every day. Guided by this theme of Focus, you need a clear destination. Lacking one, your life and your work can quickly become frustrating. And so each year, each month and even each week, you set goals. These goals then serve as your compass, helping you determine priorities and make the necessary corrections to get back on course. Your Focus is powerful because it forces you to filter; you instinctively evaluate whether or not a particular action will help you move toward your goal. Those that don't are ignored. In the end, then, your Focus forces you to be efficient. Naturally, the flip side of this is that it causes you to become impatient with delays, obstacles and even tangents, no matter how intriguing they appear to be. This makes you an extremely valuable team member. When others start to wander down other avenues, you bring them back to the main road. Your Focus reminds everyone that if something is not helping you move toward your destination, then it is not important. And if it is not important, then it is not worth your time. You keep everyone on point.

Futuristic®: "Wouldn't it be great if ..." You are the kind of person who loves to peer over the horizon. The future fascinates you. As if it were projected on the wall, you see in detail what the future might hold, and this detailed picture keeps pulling you forward, into tomorrow. While the exact content of the picture will depend on your other strengths and interests — a better product, a better team, a better life or a better world — it will always be inspirational to you. You are a dreamer who sees visions of what could be and who cherishes those visions. When the present proves too frustrating and the people around you too pragmatic, you conjure up your visions of the future, and they energize you. They can energize others too. In fact, very often people look to you to describe your visions of the future. They want a picture that can raise their sights and thereby their spirits. You can paint it for them. Practice. Choose your words carefully. Make the picture as vivid as possible. People will want to latch on to the hope you bring.

Harmony®: You look for areas of agreement. In your view, there is little to be gained from conflict and friction, so you seek to hold these to a minimum. When you know that the people around you hold differing views, you try to find the common ground. You try to steer them away from confrontation and toward harmony. In fact, harmony is one of your guiding values. You can't quite believe how much time is wasted by people trying to impose their views on others. Wouldn't we all be more productive if we kept our opinions in check and instead looked for consensus and support? You believe we would, and you live by that belief. When others are sounding off about their goals, their claims and their fervently held opinions, you hold your peace. When others strike out in a direction, you will, in the service of harmony, willingly modify your own objectives to merge with theirs (as long as their basic values do not clash with yours). When others start to argue about their pet theory or concept, you steer clear of the debate, preferring to talk about practical, down-to-earth matters on which you can all agree. In your view, we are all in the same boat, and we need this boat to get where we are going. It is a good boat. There is no need to rock it just to show that you can.

Ideation®: You are fascinated by ideas. What is an idea? An idea is a concept, the best explanation of the most events. You are delighted when you discover beneath the complex surface an elegantly simple concept to explain why things are the way they are. An idea is a connection. Yours is the kind of mind that is always looking for connections, and so you are intrigued when seemingly disparate phenomena can be linked by an obscure connection. An idea is a new perspective on familiar challenges. You revel in taking the world we all know and turning it around so we can view it from a strange but strangely enlightening angle. You love all these ideas because they are profound, because they are novel, because they are clarifying, because they are contrary and because they are bizarre. For all these reasons, you derive a jolt of energy whenever a new idea occurs to you. Others may label you creative or original or conceptual or even smart. Perhaps you are all of these. Who can be sure? What you are sure of is that ideas are thrilling. And on most days, this is enough.

Includer®: "Stretch the circle wider." This is the philosophy around which you orient your life. You want to include people and make them feel part of the group. In direct contrast to those who are drawn only to exclusive groups, you actively avoid those groups that exclude others. You want to expand the group so that as many people as possible can benefit from its support. You hate the sight of someone on the outside looking in. You want to draw them in so that they can feel the warmth of the group. You are an instinctively accepting person. Regardless of race or sex or nationality or personality or faith, you cast few judgments. Judgments can hurt a person's feelings. Why do that if you don't have to? Your accepting nature does not necessarily rest on a belief that each of us is different and that one should respect these differences. Rather, it rests on your conviction that fundamentally we are all the same. We are all equally important. Thus, no one should be ignored. Each of us should be included. It is the least we all deserve.

Individualization®: Your Individualization theme leads you to be intrigued by the unique qualities of each person. You are impatient with generalizations or "types" because you don't want to obscure what is special and distinct about each person. Instead, you focus on the differences between individuals. You instinctively observe each person's style, each person's motivation, how each thinks and how each builds relationships. You hear the one-of-a-kind stories in each person's life. This theme explains why you pick your friends just the right birthday gift, why you know that one person prefers praise in public and another detests it, and why you tailor your teaching style to accommodate one person's need to be shown and another's desire to "figure it out as I go." Because you are such a keen observer of other people's strengths, you can draw out the best in each person. This Individualization theme also helps you build productive teams. While some search for the perfect team "structure" or "process," you know instinctively that the secret to great teams is casting by individual strengths so that everyone can do a lot of what they do well.

Input®: You are inquisitive. You collect things. You might collect information — words, facts, books and quotations — or you might collect tangible objects such as butterflies, baseball cards, porcelain dolls or sepia photographs. Whatever you collect, you collect it because it interests you. And yours is the kind of mind that finds so many things interesting. The world is exciting precisely because of its infinite variety and complexity. If you read a great deal, it is not necessarily to refine your theories, but rather to add more information to your archives. If you like to travel, it is because each new location offers novel artifacts and facts. These can be acquired and then stored away. Why are they worth storing? At the time of storing, it is often hard to say exactly when or why you might need them, but who knows when they might become useful? With all those possible uses in mind, you really don't feel comfortable throwing anything away. So you keep acquiring and compiling and filing stuff away. It's interesting. It keeps your mind fresh. And perhaps one day, some of it will prove valuable.

Intellection®: You like to think. You like mental activity. You like exercising the "muscles" of your brain, stretching them in multiple directions. This need for mental activity may be focused; for example, you may be trying to solve a problem or develop an idea or understand another person's feelings. The exact focus will depend on your other strengths. On the other hand, this mental activity may very well lack focus. The theme of Intellection does not dictate what you are thinking about; it simply describes that you like to think. You are the kind of person who enjoys your time alone because it is your time for musing and reflection. You are introspective. In a sense, you are your own best companion, as you pose yourself questions and try out answers on yourself to see how they sound. This introspection may lead you to a slight sense of discontent as you compare what you are actually doing with all the thoughts and ideas that your mind conceives. Or this intro-spection may tend toward more pragmatic matters such as the events of the day or a conversation that you plan to have later. Wherever it leads you, this mental hum is one of the constants of your life.

Learner®: You love to learn. The subject matter that interests you most will be determined by your other themes and experiences, but whatever the subject, you will always be drawn to the process of learning. The process, more than the content or the result, is especially exciting for you. You are energized by the steady and deliberate journey from ignorance to competence. The thrill of the first few facts, the early efforts to recite or practice what you have learned, the growing confidence of a skill mastered — this is the process that entices you. Your excitement leads you to engage in adult learning experiences — yoga or piano lessons or graduate classes. It enables you to thrive in dynamic work environments where you are asked to take on short project assignments and are expected to learn a lot about the new subject matter in a short period of time and then move on to the next one. This Learner theme does not necessarily mean that you seek to become the subject matter expert or that you are striving for the respect that accompanies a professional or academic credential. The outcome of the learning is less significant than the "getting there."

Maximizer®: Excellence, not average, is your measure. Taking something from below average to slightly above average takes a great deal of effort and in your opinion is not very rewarding. Transforming something strong into something superb takes just as much effort but is much more thrilling. Strengths, whether yours or someone else's, fascinate you. Like a diver after pearls, you search them out, watching for the telltale signs of a strength. A glimpse of untutored excellence, rapid learning, a skill mastered without recourse to steps — all these are clues that a strength may be in play. And having found a strength, you feel compelled to nurture it, refine it and stretch it toward excellence. You polish the pearl until it shines. This natural sorting of strengths means that others see you as discriminating. You choose to spend time with people who appreciate your particular strengths. Likewise, you are attracted to others who seem to have found and cultivated their own strengths. You tend to avoid those who want to fix you and make you well-rounded. You don't want to spend your life bemoaning what you lack. Rather, you want to capitalize on the gifts with which you are blessed. It's more fun. It's more productive. And, counterintuitively, it is more demanding.

Positivity®: You are generous with praise, quick to smile and always on the lookout for the positive in the situation. Some call you light-hearted. Others just wish that their glass were as full as yours seems to be. But either way, people want to be around you. Their world looks better around you because your enthusiasm is contagious. Lacking your energy and optimism, some find their world drab with repetition or, worse, heavy with pressure. You seem to find a way to lighten their spirit. You inject drama into every project. You celebrate every achievement. You find ways to make everything more exciting and more vital. Some cynics may reject your energy, but you are rarely dragged down. Your Positivity won't allow it. Somehow you can't quite escape your conviction that it is good to be alive, that work can be fun and that no matter what the setbacks, one must never lose one's sense of humor.

Relator®: Relator describes your attitude toward your relationships. In simple terms, the Relator theme pulls you toward people you already know. You do not necessarily shy away from meeting new people — in fact, you may have other themes that cause you to enjoy the thrill of turning strangers into friends — but you do derive a great deal of pleasure and strength from being around your close friends. You are comfortable with intimacy. Once the initial connection has been made, you deliberately encourage a deepening of the relation-ship. You want to understand their feelings, their goals, their fears and their dreams, and you want them to understand yours. You know that this kind of closeness implies a certain amount of risk — you might be taken advantage of — but you are willing to accept that risk. For you, a relationship has value only if it is genuine. And the only way to know that is to entrust yourself to the other person. The more you share with each other, the more you risk together. The more you risk together, the more each of you proves your caring is genuine. These are your steps toward real friendship, and you take them willingly.

Responsibility®: Your Responsibility theme forces you to take psychological ownership for anything you commit to, and whether large or small, you feel emotionally bound to follow it through to completion. Your good name depends on it. If for some reason you cannot deliver, you automatically start to look for ways to make it up to the other person. Apologies are not enough. Excuses and rationalizations are totally unacceptable. You will not quite be able to live with yourself until you have made restitution. This conscientiousness, this near obsession for doing things right, and your impeccable ethics combine to create your reputation: utterly dependable. When assigning new responsibilities, people will look to you first because they know it will get done. When people come to you for help — and they soon will — you must be selective. Your willingness to volunteer may sometimes lead you to take on more than you should.

Restorative™: You love to solve problems. Whereas some are dismayed when they encounter yet another breakdown, you can be energized by it. You enjoy the challenge of analyzing the symptoms, identifying what is wrong and finding the solution. You may prefer practical problems or conceptual ones or personal ones. You may seek out specific kinds of problems that you have met many times before and that you are confident you can fix. Or you may feel the greatest push when faced with complex and unfamiliar problems. Your exact preferences are determined by your other themes and experiences. But what is certain is that you enjoy bringing things back to life. It is a wonderful feeling to identify the undermining factor(s), eradicate them and restore something to its true glory. Intuitively, you know that without your intervention, this thing — this machine, this technique, this person, this company — might have ceased to function. You fixed it, resuscitated it, rekindled its vitality. Phrasing it the way you might, you saved it.

Self-Assurance®: Self-Assurance is similar to self-confidence. In the deepest part of you, you have faith in your strengths. You know that you are able — able to take risks, able to meet new challenges, able to stake claims and, most important, able to deliver. But Self-Assurance is more than just self-confidence. Blessed with the theme of Self-Assurance, you have confidence not only in your abilities but in your judgment. When you look at the world, you know that your perspective is unique and distinct. And because no one sees exactly what you see, you know that no one can make your decisions for you. No one can tell you what to think. They can guide. They can suggest. But you alone have the authority to form conclusions, make decisions and act. This authority, this final accountability for the living of your life, does not intimidate you. On the contrary, it feels natural to you. No matter what the situation, you seem to know what the right decision is. This theme lends you an aura of certainty. Unlike many, you are not easily swayed by someone else's arguments, no matter how persuasive they may be. This Self-Assurance may be quiet or loud, depending on your other themes, but it is solid. It is strong. Like the keel of a ship, it withstands many different pressures and keeps you on your course.

Significance®: You want to be very significant in the eyes of other people. In the truest sense of the word, you want to be recognized. You want to be heard. You want to stand out. You want to be known. In particular, you want to be known and appreciated for the unique strengths you bring. You feel a need to be admired as credible, professional and successful. Likewise, you want to associate with others who are credible, professional and successful. And if they aren't, you will push them to achieve until they are. Or you will move on. An independent spirit, you want your work to be a way of life rather than a job, and in that work, you want to be given free rein, the leeway to do things your way. Your yearnings feel intense to you, and you honor those yearnings. And so your life is filled with goals, achievements or qualifications that you crave. Whatever your focus — and each person is distinct — your Significance theme will keep pulling you upward, away from the mediocre toward the exceptional. It is the theme that keeps you reaching.

Strategic®: The Strategic theme enables you to sort through the clutter and find the best route. It is not a skill that can be taught. It is a distinct way of thinking, a special perspective on the world at large. This perspective allows you to see patterns where others simply see complexity. Mindful of these patterns, you play out alternative scenarios, always asking, "What if this happened? OK, well what if this happened?" This recurring question helps you see around the next corner. There you can evaluate accurately the potential obstacles. Guided by where you see each path leading, you start to make selections. You discard the paths that lead nowhere. You discard the paths that lead straight into resistance. You discard the paths that lead into a fog of confusion. You cull and make selections until you arrive at the chosen path — your strategy. Armed with your strategy, you strike forward. This is your Strategic theme at work: "What if?" Select. Strike.

Woo®: Woo stands for winning others over. You enjoy the challenge of meeting new people and getting them to like you. Strangers are rarely intimidating to you. On the contrary, strangers can be energizing. You are drawn to them. You want to learn their names, ask them questions and find some area of common interest so that you can strike up a conversation and build rapport. Some people shy away from starting up conversations because they worry about running out of things to say. You don't. Not only are you rarely at a loss for words, you actually enjoy initiating with strangers because you derive satisfaction from breaking the ice and making a connection. Once that connection is made, you are quite happy to wrap it up and move on. There are new people to meet, new rooms to work, new crowds to mingle in. In your world there are no strangers, only friends you haven't met yet — lots of them.

Notes:
_____

Notes:

Notes:

Notes:

Notes:

Notes:

CPSIA information can be obtained
at www.ICGtesting.com
Printed in the USA
LVHW051111131118
596831LV00005B/544/P